DISEASES & DISORDERS

Cerebral Palsy

Barbara Sheen

LUCENT BOOKS

A part of Gale, Cengage Learning

GALE
CENGAGE Learning·

Detroit • New York • San Francisco • New Haven, Conn • Waterville, Maine • London

LIBRARY OF CONGRESS CATALOGING-IN-PUBLICATION DATA

Sheen, Barbara.
  Cerebral palsy / by Barbara Sheen.
    p. cm. -- (Diseases & disorders)
  Includes bibliographical references and index.
  ISBN 978-1-4205-0836-9 (hardcover)
  1. Cerebral palsy--Juvenile literature. I. Title.
  RC388.S436 2012
  616.8'36--dc23

                                                        2012004458

Lucent Books
27500 Drake Rd.
Farmington Hills, MI 48331

ISBN-13: 978-1-4205-0836-9
ISBN-10: 1-4205-0836-9

Printed in the United States of America
1 2 3 4 5 6 7 16 15 14 13 12

Table of Contents

"The Most Difficult Puzzles Ever Devised"

Charles Best, one of the pioneers in the search for a cure for diabetes, once explained what it is about medical research that intrigued him so. "It's not just the gratification of knowing one is helping people," he confided, "although that probably is a more heroic and selfless motivation. Those feelings may enter in, but truly, what I find best is the feeling of going toe to toe with nature, of trying to solve the most difficult puzzles ever devised. The answers are there somewhere, those keys that will solve the puzzle and make the patient well. But how will those keys be found?"

Since the dawn of civilization, nothing has so puzzled people—and often frightened them, as well—as the onset of illness in a body or mind that had seemed healthy before. A seizure, the inability of a heart to pump, the sudden deterioration of muscle tone in a small child—being unable to reverse such conditions or even to understand why they occur was unspeakably frustrating to healers. Even before there were names for such conditions, even before they were understood at all, each was a reminder of how complex the human body was, and how vulnerable.

While our grappling with understanding diseases has been frustrating at times, it has also provided some of humankind's most heroic accomplishments. Alexander Fleming's accidental discovery in 1928 of a mold that could be turned into penicillin has resulted in the saving of untold millions of lives. The isolation of the enzyme insulin has reversed what was once a death sentence for anyone with diabetes. There have been great strides in combating conditions for which there is not yet a cure, too. Medicines can help AIDS patients live longer, diagnostic tools such as mammography and ultrasounds can help doctors find tumors while they are treatable, and laser surgery techniques have made the most intricate, minute operations routine.

This "toe-to-toe" competition with diseases and disorders is even more remarkable when seen in a historical continuum. An astonishing amount of progress has been made in a very short time. Just two hundred years ago, the existence of germs as a cause of some diseases was unknown. In fact, it was less than 150 years ago that a British surgeon named Joseph Lister had difficulty persuading his fellow doctors that washing their hands before delivering a baby might increase the chances of a healthy delivery (especially if they had just attended to a diseased patient)!

Each book in Lucent's Diseases and Disorders series explores a disease or disorder and the knowledge that has been accumulated (or discarded) by doctors through the years. Each book also examines the tools used for pinpointing a diagnosis, as well as the various means that are used to treat or cure a disease. Finally, new ideas are presented—techniques or medicines that may be on the horizon.

Frustration and disappointment are still part of medicine, for not every disease or condition can be cured or prevented. But the limitations of knowledge are being pushed outward constantly; the "most difficult puzzles ever devised" are finding challengers every day.

Reaching Their Potential

Megan is a middle school student. She is also an artist whose computer-based artwork has sold for thousands of dollars. Megan has cerebral palsy. She cannot speak or control the muscles in her hands. In order to draw, she uses a special assistive device that allows her to manipulate the computer mouse with her eye movements. Because of her disability, when Megan first decided to become an artist some people said it was impossible. But Megan believed in herself. Like many individuals with cerebral palsy, she would not let her condition or misconceptions surrounding it limit her success.

A Condition That Affects Muscle Control

Cerebral palsy is a group of disorders of the brain's motor centers that affects a person's muscle control. People with cerebral palsy may have problems speaking, swallowing, and controlling their balance, coordination, movements, and/or posture. "I'm able to talk (although not plainly) and use my feet," Robert Reid, a minister with cerebral palsy, explains, "but I'm in a wheelchair [due to balance issues] and can't use my hands."[1]

Approximately 15 million people worldwide have cerebral palsy, including about eight hundred thousand in the United States. About eight thousand new cases are diagnosed in the

United States each year. Cerebral palsy affects both sexes and all ethnic and socioeconomic groups. It is found throughout the world and is the most common disabling condition in children.

Misconceptions

Having difficulties controlling one's muscles impacts every aspect of an individual's life. Besides dealing with problems that result from being physically disabled, people with cerebral palsy also have to deal with the way others treat them. Children with the condition, for example, are often teased and bullied because their peers do not understand why they move or speak differently. "Kids in school would point at me and laugh. . . . I was teased, shamed, and forced to grow a thick skin at an early age,"[2] recalls John W. Quinn, a retired U.S. Navy chief petty officer with cerebral palsy.

Jerky movements, mobility issues, and speech problems cause other misunderstandings and misconceptions, too. Although some people with cerebral palsy are mentally challenged, most are of average or above-average intelligence. Their symptoms, however, often cause misinformed individuals to misjudge them. Christine Komoroski-McCohnell, a college professor with cerebral palsy, has dealt with this misconception throughout her life. "The school officials and educators assumed that because I had CP [cerebral palsy] I must have a low IQ and no problem solving skills. . . . It has always unnerved me to have folks not recognize my fairly obvious intelligence,"[3] she explains.

This same lack of understanding of what cerebral palsy is and how it affects the body can lead others to put limits on what people with cerebral palsy can do. When individuals are repeatedly told that they cannot do something, it can lower their self-confidence and cause them emotional distress. Reid recalls:

> My uncles and aunts were oblivious that I could understand their conversations. They would talk openly about me while I was in the same room. I often heard them

say, "Why in the world are you struggling to keep Robert at home with his handicap? You know he will never be worth anything." . . . They would then give my mother advice about putting me in an institution or nursing home. . . . Their words stung.[4]

Some people with cerebral palsy accept such predictions as fact. As a result, they never reach their full potential. Others, like Jan Brunstrom, a medical doctor and martial arts expert

Cerebral palsy is a group of disorders of the brain's motor center that affects a person's muscle control. It can cause problems in speaking, swallowing, and balance coordination.

with cerebral palsy, rail against these limitations. Doing so, however, is not easy. She explains: "All my life people told me what I couldn't do. They said I'd never walk, but I did. They said I didn't belong in school, but I graduated high school as valedictorian at sixteen and went on to become a pediatric neurologist. They thought I'd never marry or have a child but I did. No one has the right to tell people with CP what they can or can't do."[5]

The Importance of Knowledge

Educating the public about what cerebral palsy is and how it affects people is the best way to destroy harmful misconceptions. Education is also the best way to support patients and their families. It can help parents of children with cerebral palsy to make wise choices about the best treatment and management of the condition. It can also make the public more sensitive to how they interact with individuals with cerebral palsy.

The more people know about cerebral palsy, the less likely that they will impose limitations on individuals with the condition. "It is easy to fear, criticize, or tease something that is unknown or makes people uncomfortable,"[6] explains Neil Matheson, a computer engineer with cerebral palsy. With the help and support of those around them, assistive technology that helps individuals cope with disabilities, and their own tenacity, people with cerebral palsy can lead happy and productive lives. They can drive, get married, own homes and businesses, go to college, and become parents, teachers, actors, artists, athletes, writers, comedians, missionaries, motivational speakers, computer programmers, and engineers, among other things. Says Komoroski-McCohnell: "I realize that my life today is as normal as anyone else's. Maybe even better. I am a soon-to-be wife. I have a college education. I am a professor of Disability Studies. I am a taxpayer, a voter, and I'm trying to compromise with my mom on plans for my wedding."[7]

Disabled but Not Unable

Some people with cerebral palsy go beyond the ordinary to the extraordinary. Among them is Christy Brown, an Irish poet, artist, and author whose life story was the basis for an Academy Award–winning movie; Jerry Traylor, the first person to jog across the United States on crutches; and Susie Maroney, a world record–holding marathon swimmer, to name just a few. Such achievements make it clear that people with cerebral palsy may be disabled, but they are not unable. With understanding and support, they can soar.

CHAPTER ONE

Understanding Cerebral Palsy

Cerebral palsy is an umbrella term for a collection of disorders that affect a person's motor system. It is caused by damage to one or more areas of the brain involved in muscle movement, coordination, and tone (the stiffness or looseness of a muscle). Whereas most people can will their bodies to move in the myriad of ways that allow them to flex and relax muscles, stand straight, walk without assistance, grasp objects, or kick a ball, for example, people with cerebral palsy are unable to control all their movements. They may have poor balance, impaired coordination, and/or abnormal movements. No two people with cerebral palsy have the same symptoms. Depending on the degree of damage, the disability a person experiences may range from minor to incapacitating.

Cerebral palsy can be treated and the symptoms lessened to some degree, but at this time, cerebral palsy cannot be cured. It is a nonprogressive static condition. This means that once individuals develop cerebral palsy, they have it for the rest of their lives. However, the movement impairment will not worsen over time. The disorder is not contagious or life threatening, and most people with cerebral palsy have a normal life expectancy.

Cerebral Palsy and the Brain

Cerebral palsy is a movement disorder of the brain. It is not a disorder of the muscles themselves or of nerves outside the

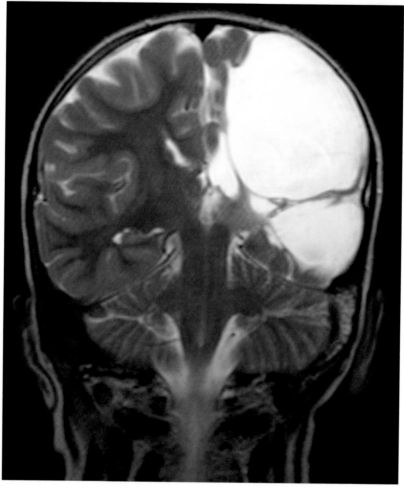

An magnetic resonance imaging (MRI) scan of the front section of a five-year-old boy with cerebral palsy. Softening of the brain due to degenerative changes in the tissue can be seen in the cream-colored area.

brain or spinal cord. It occurs when damage to developing cells in the brain's motor centers interferes with the brain's ability to communicate with and control particular muscles. Brain cells begin developing shortly after conception and continue doing so until age three. Damage to developing brain cells that results in cerebral palsy can occur before, during, or after birth, up to age three.

In order to better understand cerebral palsy, it is important to understand the brain's role in muscle control and movement. Scientists divide the brain into three main sections: the forebrain, the midbrain, and the hindbrain. The hindbrain and the forebrain house the brain's motor centers. The hindbrain is made up of the upper part of the spinal cord, the brain stem, and the cerebellum. The cerebellum coordinates balance and the sequence and duration of movement. If cells in the cerebellum are damaged, individuals may have difficulty maintaining their balance and may fall down easily. In terms of movement, when they try to grasp an object, for example, their hands may start moving late, move unsteadily, and either stop or overshoot their target. John W. Quinn recalls how this affected him:

> [The problem] was most apparent when I tried to do something athletic, like catch a football. . . . In my mind, I would make a grand leap, snatching the pigskin in midair and immediately running for the makeshift goal. The reality was quite different. By the time I got my arms up to make the grab, the ball was already over my head. The time it took my brain to process a thought and my body to take action seemed to take forever. It's almost as if I was using a cumbersome dial-up modem while everyone else utilized lightning-fast broadband. I would get so frustrated because I had a quick mind, but I was trapped in a body that was constantly slowing me down.[8]

The forebrain is also instrumental in movement. It is the largest part of the brain. It is made up of the cerebrum and structures hidden beneath it. The cerebrum is split into two equally sized hemispheres, each of which is divided into four sections, or lobes. Each lobe is involved in different physical and mental activities. The brain's motor cortex, which helps control voluntary movement, is located inside the frontal lobe. Neurons carry messages between the motor cortex and cerebellum concerning the force, duration, and direction of movement. The basal ganglia, a network of neurons hidden

Medical Problems Associated with Cerebral Palsy

Events in the brain that cause cerebral palsy to develop can also damage other parts of the brain. As a result, some people with cerebral palsy suffer from associated disorders of the brain. For example, one-half of all children with cerebral palsy have seizure disorders. Seizures occur when bursts of abnormal electrical activity in the brain interfere with normal brain functions. Other associated disorders include visual impairments, hearing loss, behavioral disorders, and learning disabilities.

Some of the symptoms of cerebral palsy, too, can cause secondary issues. Tight muscles and poor posture can cause spinal deformities. Because bones tend to be thinner and weaker when they are not walked on, people with cerebral palsy who are confined to wheelchairs are susceptible to bone fractures.

People whose face, head, and neck are affected by cerebral palsy may be unable to coordinate their swallowing. This can cause excessive drooling. About 35 percent of people with cerebral palsy drool significantly.

deep in the cerebrum, also exchanges messages with the motor cortex that trigger and regulate movement. Finally, messages are sent up and down the spinal cord between the brain and the muscles. When developing brain cells involved in movement are damaged, cerebral palsy may occur. Interestingly, since signals between the brain and the body crisscross on their way to and from the brain, the right cerebral hemisphere controls the left side of the body, and vice versa. So people with damage to the motor cortex in the right hemisphere of the cerebrum will have problems in their left limbs, and vice versa.

Prenatal Causes

Approximately 70 percent of all cerebral palsy cases are caused by events that damage the normal development of brain cells before birth. Fetal brain cells are fragile. Any number of events can threaten their normal development. Random errors that occur for no apparent reasons can cause them to develop improperly. Exposure to harmful substances can also harm developing brain cells. Since any substance that enters a pregnant woman's bloodstream is transmitted to the fetus through the placenta, the organ that carries oxygen and food to the fetus, a developing fetus is exposed to everything that enters the mother's blood, whether by mouth, air, or intravenously. Toxins such as mercury, illegal drugs, contaminated food, and infectious agents can all damage developing brain cells.

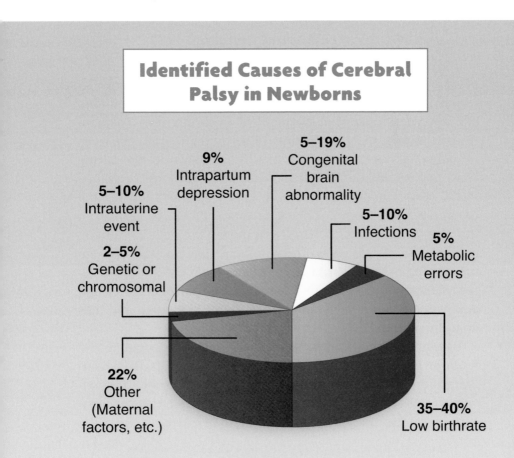

Identified Causes of Cerebral Palsy in Newborns

5–10%
Intrauterine event

2–5%
Genetic or chromosomal

9%
Intrapartum depression

5–19%
Congenital brain abnormality

5–10%
Infections

5%
Metabolic errors

35–40%
Low birthrate

22%
Other (Maternal factors, etc.)

Taken from: Centers for Disease Control and Prevention. www.cdc.gov.

Infectious agents, in particular, have been linked to the development of cerebral palsy. Maternal urinary tract infections, infections of the reproductive system, and infections of the placental membrane appear to cause damage to the developing brain's motor center. The herpes simplex virus, which causes chicken pox, cold sores, and genital herpes, and the rubella virus, which causes German measles, have also been linked to cerebral palsy. However, these infections only present a risk to the fetus if the mother contracts them for the first time during pregnancy. And, even in these cases, not all fetuses that are exposed to these viruses develop cerebral palsy. Scientists think genetic factors may make some fetuses more susceptible to abnormal brain cell development than others when they are exposed to these viruses. But little is known about what these factors may be.

Causes During and After Birth

Other cases of cerebral palsy are caused by damage to brain cells during or after birth. Lack of oxygen during birth can lead to cerebral palsy. The brain depends on a constant supply of oxygen to function normally. If the brain receives insufficient oxygen, even for a short time, delicate brain cells can be damaged. Lack of oxygen most commonly occurs during birth because of the length of labor or because of problems in the birth canal that restrict a baby's oxygen supply, such as placental abruption, the separation of the placenta from the uterus. That is what happened during the birth of Tekkla, a girl with cerebral palsy. Her mother explains: "My placenta broke prematurely. I was home alone when the major bleeding occurred and had to call the ambulance myself. . . . When she was delivered she was not breathing by herself and was completely blue."[9]

Bleeding in the brain or a stroke, which can occur in the fetus or in newborn infants around the time of birth, is also linked to cerebral palsy. Scientists do not know why this occurs, but they do know that bleeding in the brain can put pressure on fragile brain cells, causing them to break.

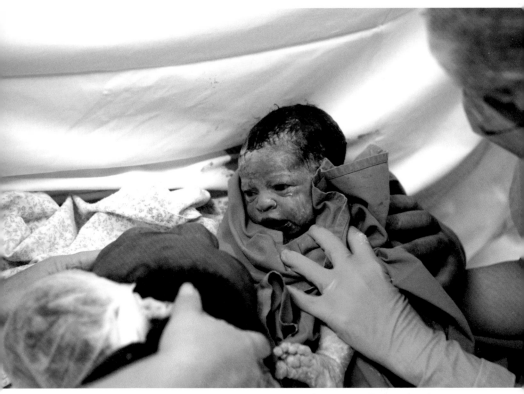

Cerebral palsy can be caused by a lack of oxygen during birth.

Another circumstance that can lead to the development of cerebral palsy occurs when babies are born with a protein in their blood, called the Rh factor, that is compatible with their father's but not their mother's blood. When this happens, the mother's blood produces powerful chemicals that attack the fetus's red blood cells, where the Rh factor is carried. If too many blood cells are destroyed, a chemical known as bilirubin can build up in the newborn baby's blood, causing severe jaundice, a condition that causes yellowing of the skin, eyes, and bodily fluids. High levels of bilirubin can damage brain cells that control movement. That is what happened to Neil Matheson. He explains: "My cerebral palsy is, in essence, the product of a 'blood war' which took place a little over forty years back at birth. My mom and dad's blood types were very incompatible together. It was this incompatibility which damaged a tiny part of my brain and as a result, I was born into this world with legs that worked a little less than perfect."[10]

Since expectant parents are screened for Rh incompatibility, and prenatal treatment is administered for at-risk pregnancies, Rh incompatibility is rarely a problem in the United States or other developed countries today. However, Rh incompatibility is a problem in developing countries, where such screening is rare.

Developing brain cells are also vulnerable to damage until age three. Head injuries that occur as a result of an accident or physical abuse can cause permanent damage to the brain, leading to the development of cerebral palsy; so can any event that causes a lack of oxygen, such as a near drowning or suffocation. Exposure to a toxic substance, such as lead, mercury, or poisons, or serious infections that cause high fever can cause damage to the motor center of the brain, too.

Risk Factors

Although anyone can develop cerebral palsy, babies that are born prematurely or in a multiple birth are at higher risk than other babies. Premature babies are quite fragile. They are often born before some of their body systems grow and develop adequately enough to function on their own. The brain and the lungs, which are both slow to develop and grow a lot during the final trimester of pregnancy, are especially vulnerable. This can cause a number of problems. For instance, inadequately developed lungs can lead to the baby receiving insufficient oxygen, which damages brain cells. Premature babies are also at greater risk of developing bleeding in the brain than full-term infants, with the highest frequency in babies with the youngest gestational age and the lowest birth weight. Indeed, the more premature the infant and the lower his or her birth weight, the more likely the baby is to develop cerebral palsy. Babies born before thirty-three weeks and weighing less than 3 pounds (1.36kg) are twenty-five to thirty times more likely to develop cerebral palsy than babies born at full term weighing more than 5 pounds (2.27kg).

Multiple-birth babies are also at risk. They often have a lower birth weight than single-birth babies of the same gestational age and are frequently born prematurely. Twins are four times more likely to develop cerebral palsy than single-birth babies. Triplets are eighteen times more likely than

Twins are four times more likely to develop cerebral palsy than single-birth babies. Triplets are eighteen times more likely.

single-birth babies. Katy, a teen with cerebral palsy, explains what happened to her:

> I was born three months prematurely as a twin (one of the most common occurrences of CP) and the doctor informed my parents that I was almost doomed to a life-long fate of wheelchairs, speech and communication problems . . . basically, all things that encompassed a worst-case scenario of CP, was what I was regarded as, by this doctor. . . . My parents were dumbfounded, probably in a state of shock for days on end . . . wondering if I was even going to survive![11]

Types of Cerebral Palsy

The way cerebral palsy affects a person depends on the part of the brain that has been damaged and the extent of the damage. As a result, the symptoms of cerebral palsy and their severity vary considerably. To better understand how an individual is affected by cerebral palsy, the condition is divided into types based on a person's symptoms. There are four possible types: spastic, athetoid, ataxic, and mixed cerebral palsy.

Spastic cerebral palsy is the most common form of the condition. It is most likely to be caused by damage to cells in the brain's motor cortex. It affects between 70 and 80 percent of all individuals with cerebral palsy. When people have spastic cerebral palsy, their muscles are stiff and tight, or hypertonic. No matter how hard they try, they are unable to relax hypertonic muscles. This can be painful and makes movement difficult. Quinn explains:

> The rigidity I experience is continuous. I don't even notice it anymore. I've had people who know about my condition ask me if I'm in pain and my answer is Zen-like—if pain is constant, is it even pain? Or is it merely my normal state of being? This perpetual tension makes all my muscles work twice as hard, resulting in my body becoming fatigued easily. When muscles are working overtime at being tight and rigid, they don't have much energy to spare.[12]

Spastic cerebral palsy can affect all four limbs as well as muscles in the head, neck, trunk, tongue, and mouth.

In addition, since stiff muscles cannot bend easily, this stiffness causes many people with spastic cerebral palsy whose legs or feet are affected to move in a lurching, scissors-like manner or to walk on their toes in much the same way as a marionette. Stiff muscles can also become so contracted that they become fixed in a rigid, abnormal position. This can cause people with cerebral palsy to have permanently clenched fists or contracted feet.

Spastic cerebral palsy can affect the muscles in any or all of the four limbs. It can also affect muscles in the head, neck, trunk, mouth, and tongue. The last two can cause difficulties speaking and/or swallowing. Medical professionals further classify spastic cerebral palsy according to the affected limbs. When only one limb is affected, the condition is known as monoplegia. If both arms or both legs are affected, the condition is known as diplegia. When one arm and one leg on one side of the body are affected, the condition is known as hemiplegia. Individuals with these three forms of spastic cerebral palsy are most likely to be able to walk. If all four limbs are involved, the condition is called quadriplegia. People with quadriplegia are the least likely to be able to walk.

People with athetoid cerebral palsy are also apt to be less ambulatory. Athetoid cerebral palsy affects about 10 percent of people with the disorder. Damage to cells in the cerebellum or the basal ganglia are often responsible for this form of cerebral palsy. It affects the whole body and causes some muscles to be stiff and others to be extremely loose, or hypotonic. This combination of tight and loose muscle tone makes it very difficult for people with athetoid cerebral palsy to control their movements. Their muscles may move involuntarily, causing their limbs to jerk, flay, or twitch uncontrollably. This seems to happen most often when individuals are startled, under stress, or feeling emotional. "I hate it when it happens because I might hit someone with my arms by accident. . . . I can't control my arms, my head, my right leg,"[13] says Wai Kin Chiu, a man with athetoid cerebral palsy.

Another 5 to 10 percent of individuals with cerebral palsy have the ataxic form. It is most often caused by damage to the cerebellum. It affects the entire body and causes problems with balance, coordination, and depth perception, as well as muscle tremors. Individuals with ataxic cerebral palsy may be unable to stand still without falling and often have problems

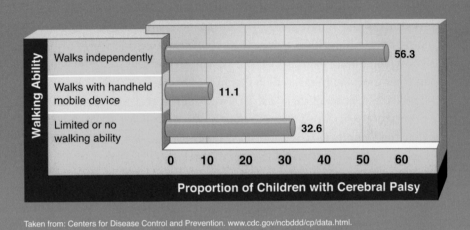

Walking Ability Among Eight-Year-Old Children with Cerebral Palsy as Tracked by the Autism and Developmental Disabilities Monitoring (ADDM) CP Network, 2006

walking. They may have trouble coordinating activities, too. Although they know how and where they want to move, making their muscles move in the desired direction is problematic. This can make activities like grasping objects, writing, feeding oneself, or scratching an itch, for example, difficult or impossible.

Some people with cerebral palsy have more than one form of the condition. This is called mixed cerebral palsy. Any of the three forms can be combined. Spastic cerebral palsy is involved in about 30 percent of mixed cases, with the most common combination being a mix of spastic and athetoid cerebral palsy.

Mild to Severe

All forms of cerebral palsy are further classified as mild, moderate, or severe, depending on the number of symptoms a person has and the severity of these symptoms. There are

Changing Views

Medical understanding of cerebral palsy has changed over time. Cerebral palsy was first mentioned in medical literature in the middle of the nineteenth century by William Little, an English surgeon. He described a condition that developed in some of his young patients. Patients with the condition had stiff, tight muscles in their arms and legs, which did not improve or worsen as they aged. Little noted that most of the affected children were born prematurely or during complicated births. Therefore, he theorized that the condition was caused during birth and was likely due to lack of oxygen. He named the condition Little's disease.

Thirty years later the psychiatrist Sigmund Freud theorized that problems in fetal brain development, not complications during birth, caused the disorder. Freud's theory was not popular. The idea that lack of oxygen during birth was the only cause of the condition continued until the 1980s. At that time, scientists looked at thirty-five thousand births in an effort to determine the cause of cerebral palsy. The scientists could not find a single cause of the disorder, which changed medical theory on the cause of cerebral palsy.

no specific guidelines for these classifications, so what is classified a mild case, for example, by one medical professional might be classified as a moderate case by another. In general, mild cases involve the least amount of brain damage and are therefore the least debilitating. Individuals with mild cases may have only minor difficulties using their muscles and may not appear disabled to the general public, although they may seem clumsy and uncoordinated. They have to exert extra effort to perform tasks or lift objects that are easy for fully abled individuals, and they fatigue easily. René Z. Milner, whose teenage daughter, Alicia, has mild cerebral palsy, explains:

It is hard to see her struggle to brush her long hair herself. It is very difficult to watch her eat without "reminding" her constantly to close her mouth when chewing, (this isn't bad manners, she literally can't seem to do it). . . . She cannot pour herself a glass of tea or water if the pitcher is near full—it is too heavy for her. She has no real coordination when it comes to PE [physical education] in school, but she tries and that is all that counts so far. She has made great strides though in one area—she plays the clarinet in band and worked so hard that she moved from 12th chair to 2nd this year. This to me is a major accomplishment!! It takes great dexterity of her fingers. The mild CP diagnosis is hard to live with when your child "appears" normal to most people. Teachers and friends wonder why she isn't able to do many physical tasks as well as she does educational tasks. . . . It has been a struggle at times to reassure her that not everyone is "coordinated" anyway.[14]

People with moderate cases may have trouble walking or using their arms. Some depend on crutches for support, whereas others use an electric scooter or a wheelchair. Severe cases are the most debilitating. They usually involve problems with all four limbs and with speech. Individuals with severe cases may be unable to walk, use their arms, speak, sit upright, or hold their neck and head erect. Monica Videnieks, a writer with severe cerebral palsy, has many of these symptoms. "I communicate with an electronic communication device. I use a motorized wheelchair which I control with pressure from the back of my head,"[15] she explains.

Clearly, cerebral palsy affects different people in different ways. In all cases, however, damage to developing cells in the brain's motor centers makes it difficult for individuals with cerebral palsy to control their muscles. No matter the severity or type, for these individuals and their families, the first step in dealing with the condition is recognizing the symptoms and treating them.

CHAPTER TWO

Diagnosis and Treatment

When a child has significant delays in developing motor skills, cerebral palsy is suspected. Once the condition is diagnosed, treatment can begin. The goal of treatment is to improve muscle tone and mobility. Treatment plans vary, depending on the patient's symptoms.

Reaching Developmental Milestones

Although every child develops at a different pace, within the first two years of life healthy babies reach a set of developmental milestones involving motor skills in a fairly predictable time frame. These milestones include lifting the head at one month; rolling over, sitting without support, and reaching and grasping at six months; crawling and holding a bottle at nine months; walking at twelve months; climbing stairs, stacking blocks, and managing a spoon at eighteen months; kicking a ball and turning book pages at twenty-four months. Children with cerebral palsy are significantly delayed in reaching these milestones.

Although these milestones are not absolutes, significant delays are red flags for parents. Marshalyn Yeargin-Allsopp, the chief of the Developmental Disabilities Branch of the Centers for Disease Control and Prevention, describes the type of delays parents should look for:

A child over 6 months might have difficulty bringing the hands together or reach with only one hand while keeping the other in a fist. A child over 10 months might crawl by pushing off with one hand and leg while dragging the opposite hand and leg or not sit by himself. A child over 12 months might not crawl or not be able to stand with support, and a child over 24 months might not be able to walk or not be able to push a toy with wheels. Parents should be particularly aware of these milestones if your child has any risk factors for CP, such as prematurity.[16]

Within their first two years of life, healthy babies reach developmental milestones. These include crawling at eight months, holding a bottle at nine months, walking at a year, and stacking blocks and climbing stairs at eighteen months. Children with cerebral palsy are significantly delayed in reaching these milestones.

Making a Diagnosis

Even with evidence of developmental delays, diagnosing cerebral palsy is not simple. There is no blood or imaging test that can positively diagnose the condition. When cerebral palsy is suspected, doctors question the parent about developmental delays. The child's physical development is compared with what is considered normal for children of the same age. The child is also examined. Doctors test the child's reflexes to see if they respond normally when they are stimulated, and they check the child's muscle tone. Finally, the child's Apgar score is reviewed. The Apgar score results from an evaluation that is conducted on babies minutes after birth. It provides a quick assessment of a newborn's health. It looks at five vital signs: the baby's color, pulse, reflexes, muscle tone, and breathing. Based on the assessment, the infant is given a score. A perfect score is a 10. Scores of at least 7 are considered healthy. Although many infants with scores below 7 never develop health issues, a low score in conjunction with developmental delays increases the possibility that the child has cerebral palsy. Generally, the lower the Apgar score, the greater the possibility.

Even if all the evidence points to cerebral palsy, before a diagnosis can be made, conditions such as muscular dystrophy, brain tumors, neurological diseases, arthritis, and certain cancers that can cause developmental delays must be eliminated. This is accomplished through various tests. What ultimately confirms the diagnosis is whether the patient's symptoms worsen. Since cerebral palsy symptoms do not get worse, monitoring patients over a few months helps doctors determine whether the cause of an individual's problems is cerebral palsy.

Individualized Treatment

Once a diagnosis is made, treatment can begin. Since no two cases of cerebral palsy are exactly alike, treatment is highly individualized. Medical professionals develop a treatment plan for each patient based on the type and severity of cerebral palsy and the muscles that are affected. Patients with tight, spastic muscles, for example, may benefit from surgery,

The Apgar Score

The Apgar score is named after Virginia Apgar, a physician who developed the index in 1952 to ensure that newborn infants receive immediate care in the critical first few minutes of life.

The score is divided into five sections whose titles—appearance (or skin color), pulse, grimace (or reflexes), activity (or muscle tone), and respiration—are based on an acronym using the letters of Apgar's name. Infants are rated 0 to 2 for each section. Under appearance, blue or gray skin color rates 0, normal color except on the extremities rates 1, and normal color over the entire body rates 2. No pulse rates 0, pulse below 100 beats per minute rates 1, and pulse over 100 rates 2. Under grimace, no response to reflex stimulation rates 0, a grimace rates 1, and sneezing, coughing, or pulling away rate 2. Under activity, no movement rates 0, arms and legs flexed rates 1, and active movement rates 2. Absent respiration rates 0, slow irregular breathing rates 1, and crying rates 2.

These scores are added together. A total score of 7 to 10 is normal. A score of 4 might require resuscitation. A score of 0 to 4 requires immediate resuscitation.

whereas those with loose muscles may not. Speech therapy is indicated for patients with problems that affect their speech or swallowing. The presence of associated health issues such as seizure disorders, which sometimes affect people with cerebral palsy, is considered and treated with medication when necessary. But no matter the specific treatment plan, treatment focuses on managing the condition by improving muscle tone and mobility. It requires a team of medical professionals working together to achieve this goal.

Physical Therapy

Physical therapy is the most frequently prescribed treatment for cerebral palsy. It is effective in relieving symptoms for all types of the disorder. Physical therapy focuses on improving gross motor skills. These are skills that involve the large muscles of the body; those in the legs, arms, back, and abdomen. Physical therapy helps develop muscle strength and tone and improves balance, posture, flexibility, stamina, and mobility.

During physical therapy, patients are given a specially designed exercise program created to meet their individual needs. The program changes as the patient's needs change. Therapy usually begins in the first few years of life, shortly after a diagnosis of cerebral palsy is made. It usually continues throughout childhood and sometimes into a patient's teen years. In physical therapy, medical professionals called physical therapists help individuals to develop better ways to move and balance, thereby helping patients gain the skills needed to sit upright, stand, walk, run, kick and throw a ball, negotiate stairs, or use an assistive device like crutches, a walker, or a wheelchair.

Sessions are held in a physical therapy center. These centers resemble an ordinary gym equipped with exercise mats and

A therapist and a boy with cerebral palsy work in a swimming pool as part of a physical therapy session.

bicycles, weight training machines, parallel bars, balance balls, and massage tables. But they are far from ordinary. They are staffed by medical professionals trained to work with people with mobility issues.

Sessions may be held one to five times per week for about an hour per session. Sessions can be difficult, painful, and exhausting. In order to achieve the best results, patients are expected to do their exercises at home, too. John W. Quinn recalls: "I was doing exercises at home every day and going to Children's Hospital for therapy twice weekly. I tried not to think about what other kids were doing. My brothers and sisters heard, 'Did you practice your piano, Susan?' or 'Michael, is your homework done?' But for months on end, all I got was, 'John did you finish your exercises today?'"[17] Since physical therapy can significantly increase an individual's mobility, most individuals say that the results are well worth the time and effort.

Occupational Therapy

Occupational therapy is another widely prescribed treatment. It is similar to physical therapy. However, occupational therapy focuses on fine motor skills, those skills that involve the small muscles of the body, like the fingers, hands, toes, feet, and mouth. This type of therapy is led by medical professionals known as occupational therapists. The goal of occupational therapy is to help people develop skills that let them function as effectively as possible in their daily lives. Dressing, bathing, grooming, feeding oneself, writing, cutting with scissors, using a computer mouse, and drawing are just a few of these skills. Occupational therapy employs activities that develop and improve control of small muscles, like stringing beads, stacking blocks, and fitting pegs in holes.

Occupational therapy also helps patients develop compensating tactics, teaching them how to use muscles they can control in place of, or in assistance of, weaker muscles. For instance, patients who cannot control their wheelchair with their hands may be taught to control it with their feet or head.

An occupational therapist assists a child in using a scissors. Occupational therapy's goal is to help people develop skills that let them function as effectively as possible in their daily lives.

In addition, occupational therapists work with families to make homes more accessible, and they help patients find the best special equipment to help make everyday living easier. This may include items like modified cups and spoons to make feeding easier or specially designed, easy-to-grip pens and pencils.

According to an article prepared by My Child, an organization that provides information and resources for the families of children with cerebral palsy:

> Occupational therapists provide skills required in daily living for those with impairment. These professionals focus on assessing and developing an individual's ability to function in normal daily activities at home, in school, out in public, and at work. The goal is to foster independence, productivity, and self-care. . . . When an individual requires environment design changes or assistive technologies at home, school, work, or play, an occupational therapist will help secure the necessary items and train the individual and his or her family how to use the equipment.[18]

Speech Therapy

Treatment for individuals whose face, mouth, neck, and/or tongue have been affected by cerebral palsy includes speech therapy. Speech therapists work with patients on special exercises designed to help them control the movement of their tongue and mouth, improve their breathing, strengthen their mouths and vocal chords, and improve their ability to produce the basic sounds that form words. Robert Reid explains how speech therapy helped him:

> My speech impediment coupled with my sporadic motions, led many people to simply ignore what I was trying to say. They thought I was too hard to understand. I was blessed to be under the care of a therapist who was the head of the speech pathology department at Texas Tech. . . . He began by having me say "ah" for about five seconds each time. This exercise helped to strengthen my vocal chords. Another exercise was drinking through a straw. At the end of every session the therapist would take a little steel ball and massage my palate with it. Then he would put his thumbs on my lips and massage my lips in

a circular motion. After he did this, my lips would burn. It was a sensation I'd never felt before, and no speech therapist has done it since. Yet, somehow these techniques changed my life. Within six months of starting the treatment, I was able to speak in a way that everyone could understand.[19]

If patients are completely unable to speak, speech therapists help them acquire special communication devices like computers with speech synthesizers that speak for them. Speech therapy also helps individuals with drooling and/or swallowing problems. Drooling is the involuntary loss of saliva from the mouth. It is caused by a lack of coordination of the muscles of the mouth, face, and neck. Patients who drool are given exercises that teach them how to better work their mouths and tongues to push saliva back toward their throats. Other exercises can help people control their ability to swallow.

Drug Therapy

In some cases drug therapy can ease cerebral palsy symptoms. A muscle relaxant known as baclofen can relax tight muscles in people with spastic cerebral palsy so that they can move more easily. Baclofen is delivered into the patient's body by a pump that is implanted under the skin of the patient's abdomen. The pump is about the size of a deck of cards. It delivers a prescribed amount of baclofen through a tiny tube into the fluid around a person's spinal cord. A computer turns the pump on and adjusts the dosage as needed. The pump must be refilled about every two months. This is done by inserting a needle through the skin and into the pump.

As with any medication, baclofen can produce side effects. Sleepiness, nausea, headaches, and dizziness are most common. These can usually be managed by adjusting the dosage. There is also a danger of infection at the implantation site. But because the medication makes it easier for individuals to move, exercise, and strengthen their muscles, many people are willing to face that risk.

Cerebral palsy patients need speech therapy exercises to help them control the movement of tongue and mouth and to improve breathing and their ability to pronounce words.

Other drugs known as anticholinergic drugs, which reduce involuntary muscle movements, are sometimes prescribed for athetoid cerebral palsy. However, these drugs are primarily used to treat Parkinson's disease. They have not been well studied in treating cerebral palsy and appear to lose their effectiveness over time.

Serial Casts

A procedure known as serial casting is another treatment option for some individuals. It uses a series of lightweight, well-padded casts to incrementally stretch contracted muscles at the hip, knee, or ankle joints, thereby giving patients greater range of motion. The cast immobilizes the joint the muscle is connected to while keeping the muscle in a stretched position. It is worn for a given period of time. Then it is removed and a new cast that increases the angle of the stretch is applied. It usually takes four to six weeks for the procedure to be completed. It is followed by physical therapy to strengthen the muscle. The casting procedure is relatively painless, and wearing the casts does not limit daily activities. In fact, the casts often provide patients with added support. Ellen, whose son Max has cerebral palsy, explains:

> The serial casting turned out to be far less of an ordeal than I thought it was going to be. . . . Max actually liked having the casts on and protested every time one had to come off. We removed each one ourselves the night before the next was due to go on. They were pretty easy to unravel. The casts did not hamper Max's style in any way—just the opposite. First, they gave him good balance (much better than that in-turning right foot) so he could get around pretty quickly with them on. . . . The serial casting did the job: His right foot is straight and staying flat on the ground when he walks.[20]

Surgery

Tight muscles can also be eased with surgery. The three most common surgeries for cerebral palsy are tenotomy, tendon transfer, and selective dorsal rhizotomy. A tenotomy and a tendon transfer help relieve tight and contracted muscles in the hips, knees, and ankles. When muscles are too tight and become contracted, the tendons that attach the muscles to the bone may also tighten. This makes it very difficult to move the muscles.

In a tenotomy, the tendon around the affected muscle is cut entirely or partially through. This allows the muscle to be stretched. Depending on the severity of the case, the surgery may be performed through the skin, which is less invasive, or by surgically exposing the tendon. The less invasive method takes only a few minutes. Patients stay awake during the procedure but feel no pain because the area around the tendon is numbed with a local anesthetic. The surgeon inserts a thin blade through the numbed skin and partially cuts the tendon in two or more places. This frees the muscles so that it can move more easily.

Doctors perform a tenotomy on a patient with a hand disorder. The procedure allows muscles to stretch, making movement easier.

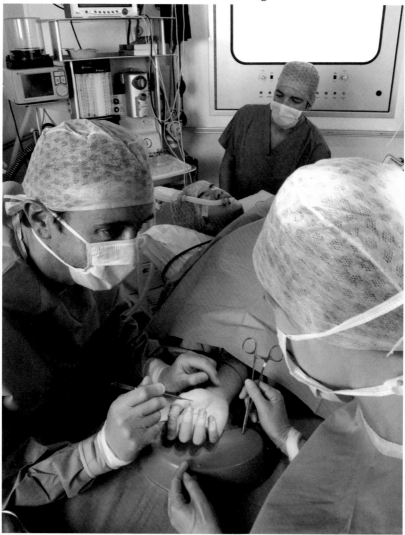

In more severe cases patients are administered general anesthetic so that they sleep through the procedure. The surgeon cuts open the area around the tendon to expose it. Then the surgeon cuts the tendon in half lengthwise. The two strips are sewn together to form a single, longer tendon. In a tendon transfer, the tendon is cut and reattached to the bone at a different point.

After the surgery, the contracted muscle is stretched. In more severe cases a cast is applied. It keeps the muscle in place while the tendon regrows. This takes two to three weeks.

Adults with Cerebral Palsy

As people with cerebral palsy age, they face many challenges that may require medical treatment. Premature aging, caused by the extra stress and strain cerebral palsy puts on the body, is one challenge. Post-impairment syndrome, a combination of pain, fatigue, and weakness due to lifelong muscle abnormalities, is another. Pain can become a chronic condition if it is not treated. Arthritis, too, may develop.

Emotional problems may also require treatment. Adults with cerebral palsy are three to four times more likely to develop depression than people without disabilities. Developing depression appears to be related not to the severity of their disabilities, but to how well they cope with them.

The National Institute of Neurological Disorders and Stroke points out the need for regular medical care for adults with cerebral palsy:

> Because of their unique medical situations, adults with cerebral palsy benefit from regular visits to their doctor and ongoing evaluation of their physical status. It is important to evaluate physical complaints to make sure they are not the result of underlying conditions. For example, adults

Depending on the location of the surgery, the cast may go from the toes to the knees or hips. Once the cast is removed, physical therapy helps strengthen the muscle. In less invasive cases, casting is not usually necessary. Instead, patients are fitted with a brace, which helps the patient to walk. As the tendon heals, the size of the brace is reduced.

A selective dorsal rhizotomy also helps relieve tight muscles. It is a surgical procedure in which selected nerve roots along the back of the spinal cord are cut in an effort to loosen muscles that send messages to those nerves. An informational

with cerebral palsy are likely to experience fatigue, but fatigue can also be due to undiagnosed medical problems that could be treated and reversed.

National Institute of Neurological Disorders and Stroke. "Cerebral Palsy: Hope Through Research." www.ninds.nih.gov/disorders/cerebral_palsy/detail_cerebral _palsy.htm#179403104.

As people with cerebral palsy age through adulthood they face many challenges that may require medical treatment and a caregiver.

brochure prepared by the Department of Neurosurgery of St. Louis Children's Hospital explains:

> Normally muscles must have enough tone to maintain posture or movement against the force of gravity, while at the same time provide flexibility and speed of movement. The command to be stiff, or increase muscle tone, goes to the spinal cord via nerves from the muscle itself. Since these nerves tell the spinal cord just how much tone the muscle has, they are called "sensory nerve fibers." The command to be flexible or reduce muscle tone comes to the spinal cord from nerves in the brain. These two commands must be well coordinated in the spinal cord for muscles to work smoothly and easily while maintaining strength. The brain of the child with cerebral palsy is . . . unable to [sufficiently] influence the amount of flexibility a muscle should have. The command from the muscle itself dominates the spinal cord and, as a result, the muscle is too stiff, or "spastic."[21]

By cutting some of these sensory nerve fibers at their root, a selective dorsal rhizotomy reduces the messages of stiffness from the muscles to better balance the messages of flexibility from the brain. As a result, muscle tone is more normal and individuals can move more easily. Indeed, with intensive physical therapy, patients who could not walk independently before the surgery are often able to walk independently within a year. The procedure takes about four hours and presents all the risks of any major surgery. And, although the surgery cannot cure cerebral palsy, the results can be life changing. This was the case for Lewis Evans, a boy with cerebral palsy. His mother explains:

> I heard about another family whose child had undergone the procedure and after a lot of thought we decided to go for it. The surgeon cut some of the nerves in Lewis's spine. . . . There was a dramatic improvement each day. By day three they got him into a wheelchair to do an hour of sitting up. Within ten days he was walking [with assistance].

. . . His legs are now relaxed and straight and he can walk with sticks without stumbling. . . . The doctor says he will be in full strength within a year and walking unaided.[22]

Currently, there is no treatment that can cure cerebral palsy. But treatments like selective dorsal rhizotomy, serial casting, muscle relaxant medication, and physical, speech, and occupational therapy can strengthen muscles and improve muscle tone. In so doing, these treatments help people with cerebral palsy move more easily, which improves the quality of their lives.

CHAPTER THREE

Supportive Therapies

In order to achieve a maximum level of muscle control and range of movement, many individuals with cerebral palsy add supportive therapies to their treatment plan. Many of these therapies are widely recognized as being effective in relieving the symptoms of cerebral palsy without presenting significant health risks. Other therapies are more controversial.

Equine Therapy

Therapeutic horseback riding, which is also known as equine therapy or hippotherapy, is a popular supportive therapy for cerebral palsy. In this type of therapy, people with cerebral palsy are supervised by specially trained instructors who teach them how to ride a horse. At first, special ropes and props may be used to keep the rider in an upright position. The instructor may ride on the horse with the patient or walk beside the horse in order to prevent falls. With practice, patients are usually able to ride on their own. The therapy presents few health risks and many benefits. It loosens tight leg and arm muscles, promotes good posture, and increases balance and muscle strength. In addition, it has been shown to improve speech. Individuals with cerebral palsy who have speech problems may be reluctant to speak because they are often misunderstood. However, a rider must vocalize in order to communicate with the horse. With practice, the patient's speech gains clarity, and he or she gains more confidence in speaking.

Equine therapy has psychological benefits, too. As riders gain control over the horse, they feel empowered. This boosts their self-esteem. At the same time, for people with mobility issues, moving freely on a horse gives them a sense of freedom from the restrictions their disability puts upon them. In addition, horseback riding is fun. It gives riders a chance to exercise in the fresh air and to bond with animals that they might

An eight-year-old with cerebral palsy takes a ride on a horse while therapists attend him. Equine therapy loosens leg and arm muscles, increases balance and muscle strength, and promotes good posture.

not otherwise get to experience. Mary C. Vrtis, a registered nurse and certified therapeutic riding instructor, describes the experience of Sam, a boy with cerebral palsy:

> While on his horse . . . Sam is free of his wheelchair. His body is moving easily in smooth movements, and the natural rhythm of the horse helps to stretch his tight muscles. His leg muscles are exercised with motions that are similar to those used in walking, increasing his flexibility and helping to prevent muscle contractures. . . . Despite the difficulty that he has communicating, the instructor and volunteers have no trouble hearing him say the word "trot," as he tells his horse to move faster. . . . The first and only time that Sam stops smiling is when the instructor tells him that the lesson is finished. Sam leans over to pat his horse to thank him for the ride.[23]

Aquatic Therapy

Like equine therapy, aquatic therapy can give people with cerebral palsy a sense of freedom as it helps strengthen their bodies. Aquatic therapy is a form of physical therapy in which individuals do specially designed exercises in water. The therapy usually takes place in a special therapy pool, where the water temperature is kept warm. This is because warm water relaxes the body and stiff muscles.

Exercising in water has many benefits for people with cerebral palsy and few health risks. It builds muscle strength, reduces muscle tightness and pain, and improves range of motion, balance, and coordination. According to Jan Vilums, a physical therapy assistant:

> The negative influence of poor balance, poor postural control, and excessive joint loading [putting excess pressure on a joint] are reduced in the water. Aquatic therapy also reduces muscle spasticity and joint pain. . . . Aquatic therapy uses the buoyancy, warmth, and variable resistance of water for patients to get exercise

of their weakened or spastic muscles. Water can provide an atmosphere of reduced body weight by up to
90%. The buoyancy of water decreases the influence of
gravity and provides increased postural support. These
characteristics may allow children with CP [cerebral
palsy] to exercise in water with more freedom than on
land. The resistive forces of [water] . . . permit a variety
of aerobic and strengthening activities that can be easily modified to accommodate the wide range of motor
abilities of children with CP.[24]

Music Therapy

Music therapy is another supportive therapy. It uses music as a
tool to help improve individuals' speech and motor skills. During music therapy sessions, a trained music therapist leads a
group of patients in activities such as singing, moving to music,
and playing instruments, structured to meet specific goals. For
example, singing is used to improve breath control as well as
speech and language skills. Moving to music is used to improve
balance, coordination, strength, and mobility. Playing instruments is used to improve fine motor skills.

These activities also provide individuals with a social activity that is fun and relaxing. It connects them with other people
and may enhance their social skills and self-esteem. Erica Cao,
who is studying music therapy, describes a music therapy session she recently observed:

> This morning, groups of three of us went to the Carter
> School for Cerebral Palsy to observe music therapy. . . .
> Each session consisted of around four students, each with
> various degrees of cerebral palsy or autism.
>
> We witnessed how music could help the students with
> movement (such as using arm movements to hit a drum
> and dance) and vocalizations (such as singing). I truly
> saw the patience and care required of music therapists,
> and how it is extremely rewarding when one is able to

reach another through music. The music therapist asked if I could help hold a [cymbal] in front of a student and match the [cymbal's] position with the student's arm movements. I desperately wanted to reach him somehow . . . and I encouraged him to hit the [cymbal] through actions and song. One wonderful moment was when one of the students started banging the drums, and the rest of us answered him by playing back his rhythm. It was amazing because he realized what we were doing, and his face lit up in understanding.[25]

Music therapy uses music as a tool to improve individuals' speech and motor skills.

Constraint-Induced Movement Therapy

Constraint-induced movement therapy is another support-ive treatment. It has been proved effective in helping stroke victims regain movement in their arms and hands and has recently gained the attention of therapists who work with individuals who have hemiplegia. The therapy focuses on improving movement of the arm or hand affected by cerebral palsy by restraining the nonaffected arm or hand. This forces the patient to use the affected body part. Constraint-induced movement therapists believe that this treatment can reverse the effects of learned nonuse of the arm or hand affected by cerebral palsy.

The therapy is based on the theory that the brain is plastic. That means the brain is able to grow and change as a result of experience. Research has shown that if certain pathways of the brain are damaged, other pathways may open up and become stronger with use. Therefore, if one area of the brain involved in muscle control is damaged, another part of the brain can take over for it. For this to happen, the affected body part must be moved repeatedly. To make sure that this is accomplished, the unaffected arm or hand may be put in a sling or a special restraint glove for up to six hours a day for anywhere between ten days to more than a month.

A number of studies have looked at the effectiveness of the therapy on children with hemiplegia. In a 2006 Columbia University study, twenty-two children with hemiplegia were divided into two groups. One group wore slings on their un-involved arms for six hours a day for ten days. While wearing the slings, the children were engaged in play involving the use of their free arm. The other group acted as the control group. In a medical study, a control group is not treated. It serves as a comparison group when the results of the treatment are evaluated. Both groups' ability to move their affected arms was measured before the therapy period, after it ended, and six months later. The children in the therapy group showed significantly improved mobility in their affected arm both after the therapy ended and six months later. The control group did

Acupuncture for Cerebral Palsy

Acupuncture is another supportive therapy for cerebral palsy. It is an ancient form of Chinese medicine. Acupuncture is based on the theory that humans have a life energy called chi flowing through their bodies. If this energy becomes blocked, illness and pain occurs. To relieve these blockages, acupuncturists insert hair-thin needles into specific points in the body to stimulate the flow of energy. This, acupuncturists believe, relieves pain, makes it easier for nerve impulses to travel back and forth between the brain and muscles, and allows an increased blood supply to reach the brain. When more blood reaches the brain, acupuncturists say, healthy brain cells are strengthened and may take over some of the functions of damaged brain cells. The result is greater muscle control and mobility and less pain.

There is little evidence in Western science that chi exists, and many Western medical professionals are skeptical that acupuncture can increase muscle control. There is evidence that acupuncture can relieve pain. And studies in China indicate that acupuncture can improve mobility in children with cerebral palsy.

Although many Western scientists reject acupuncture as a way to increase muscle control, studies in China indicate that acupuncture can improve mobility in children with cerebral palsy.

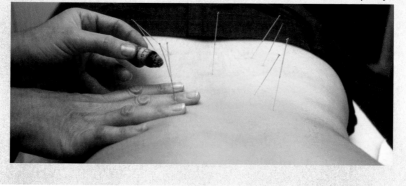

not. A similar 2007 study at the Karolinska Institute in Stockholm, Sweden, looked at the effect of wearing a restraint glove on twenty-one children with hemiplegia while they played for two hours a day for two months. Once again, the therapy group showed improved mobility over the control group. Other studies, too, have yielded promising results.

Despite such results, some health experts are concerned that the therapy may be confusing and frustrating for young patients, causing psychological issues. It may also delay their mental development by slowing down their already limited ability to play and explore. These matters were not an issue for Ben, a twenty-eight-year-old man with hemiplegia of his left side. He underwent a form of constraint-induced therapy in 2010. Before the therapy he was unable to perform simple, two-handed tasks like buttoning his pants, cutting food, or tying his shoes and therefore was unable to function independently. But after a year of weekly constraint-induced movement therapy, Ben gained enough mobility in his left hand to do all these tasks. As a result, he was able to move into his own apartment. He has also started learning to play guitar, a lifelong dream that seemed unattainable in the past. When asked how he felt about the results of the therapy, he said that he was "really surprised, I didn't think I would ever be able to use my left hand. Who knows—maybe I'll be able to play music yet!"[26]

Botox Treatments

Botox is a drug made from the *Clostridium botulinum* bacteria. It is a powerful toxin that blocks transmissions between nerves and muscles. It also can cause a deadly form of food poisoning known as botulism. Although it is a dangerous substance, scientists have found that, in minute doses, Botox can be used as a medication. It is approved by the U.S. Food and Drug Administration (FDA) as a treatment for facial wrinkles. The FDA is a government regulatory agency that ensures medications are safe and effective for specific purposes. Medications approved by the FDA for one purpose can be prescribed for other purposes at a doctor's discretion. This is known as an off-label use of a drug. Increasingly, Botox is being prescribed as an off-label treatment to relieve tight muscles caused by cerebral palsy.

The treatment involves injecting Botox directly into tight, spastic muscles with a small, thin needle. Almost any muscle can be injected. However, since only a tiny amount of the toxin can be used safely, usually no more than two or three muscles are injected at once. A few minutes before the procedure, the injection sites are numbed with medication. Very young children may be given an anesthetic. Once the Botox enters the muscles, it blocks the transmission of nerve impulses that cause the muscles to tighten. As a result, the muscles relax. This effect lasts three to six months, after which the treatment must be repeated. Treatment is followed by physical therapy that focuses on stretching and strengthening the loosened muscles.

For unknown reasons, Botox treatment is not effective on all patients, and it sometimes works early on but loses its effectiveness after a few treatments. For those individuals that it helps, however, the results can be remarkable. Tara responded to an article about the treatment on a blog about children with cerebral palsy. She explains how it helped her son Daniel:

> My son, aged 5, has received five rounds of botox in his legs and, overall, I've been thrilled with the results. The decrease in tone [loosening of the muscles] has allowed him some much-needed relief from such continuous tightness, and with each round, he was able to make some rather large functional leaps. After his first round, he started crawling on all fours; after his second, he started crawling up the stairs, after his third, he was able to put himself into a sitting position, and after his fourth, he started functionally walking with his reverse walker [a walker in which the frame and wheels are behind the user and the front is open]. With rather obsessive stretching, and increased therapy, he has managed to retain the function, even after the botox wears off.[27]

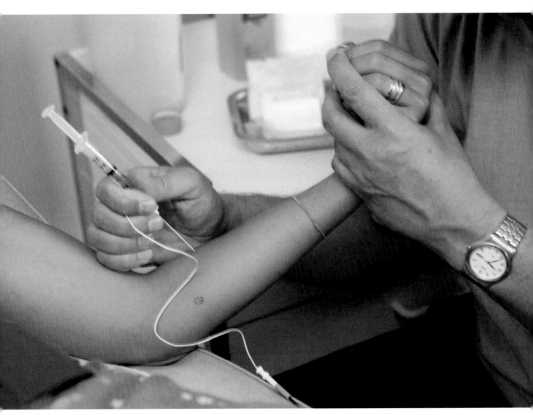

Botox injections into tight, spastic muscles block the transmission of nerve impulses that cause muscles to tighten.

Despite such results, Botox treatment for cerebral palsy is controversial. Botox is a poison, and introducing it into the body is risky. Scientists do not know what effect long-term use of Botox may have on the muscles. In addition, because it is administered off-label, determining where it is injected and how much is administered is not an exact science. There is no set dosage; the dosage is determined by the doctor. Establishing the correct dose in young children is especially tricky because of their low body weight. If the dosage is too small, it may be ineffective. If it is too large, the toxin can spread to areas distant from the injection site, leading to serious health problems such as difficulty swallowing, respiratory issues, and pneumonia. In 2007 a little girl with cerebral palsy went into

The Paralympics

The Paralympics is the second-largest sporting event in the world. Started in 1960, the Paralympics is a shortened term for Parallel Olympics. The Paralympics feature world-class wheelchair, amputee, cerebral palsy, and blind/visually impaired athletes. The Paralympics are governed by the International Paralympics Committee, which is a member of the International Olympics Committee. The games follow the Olympic Games in the same host city. There are both Summer and Winter Paralympic Games.

Athletes are male and female. They represent almost every country in the world. Thirty-nine hundred athletes from 146 countries participated in the 2008 Paralympics in Beijing. Only the highest-achieving athletes can participate. Athletes must qualify for events along similar guidelines as those for the Olympics. The athletes are grouped in classes defined by their degree of disability. Athletes of the same class compete against each other. There are twenty Paralympic sports in the Summer Games and five in the Winter. Events include Alpine skiing, cross-country skiing, biathlon, power lifting, swimming, shooting, track and field, bocce, and wheelchair dancing, among other sports.

A para-athlete celebrates a bronze medal win at the 2008 Paralympics in China. Thirty-nine hundred athletes from 146 countries participated.

respiratory failure and died after a Botox injection. Although it was not proved, her parents believed that an overdose of Botox caused her death.

Parents of children with cerebral palsy do not take lightly the decision to treat their offspring with Botox. Ellen, whose son has cerebral palsy, explains: "My heart aches for this mother [whose daughter died from Botox], whose grief must surely be laced with so much anger, perhaps even guilt. Botox was supposed to improve her child's life; instead, it might have killed her. If you're a mom of a kid with special needs you know just what it's like to want to do something, anything, to help your child, enable him [to] function, allow him to live a life less challenged."[28]

Cord Blood Infusions

A cord blood infusion is another controversial supportive treatment for cerebral palsy. Because there have not been controlled studies on humans conclusively proving its effectiveness, it is considered to be an experimental treatment. Still, many parents of children with cerebral palsy are seeking it out.

A cord blood infusion for cerebral palsy involves patients receiving a transfusion of their own umbilical cord blood. The blood is administered intravenously through the patient's arms or legs. The blood contains stem cells, cells that are capable of changing into and repairing any cell in the body. Using a patient's umbilical cord blood to treat cerebral palsy is based on the theory that the transfused stem cells will travel to the brain and repair or replace damaged cells involved in cerebral palsy.

Typically, after birth, umbilical cords are discarded. Some parents, however, are opting to collect the cord blood after the umbilical cord is cut and deposit the blood in a cord blood bank. There the blood is preserved in case the stem cells are needed to treat disease in the future. There are both public and private cord banks. Public cord banks accept donations of umbilical cord blood to be used by anyone in need. Donors cannot retrieve their donation in the future. On the other hand, donors retain possession of cord blood stored in private cord banks. They can retrieve it at any time, if it is needed in the future to treat the donor baby. Private cord banks are for-profit businesses. They charge a fee to preserve and store cord blood. They have been criticized for aggressive marketing campaigns that portray cord blood as a miracle cure.

A nurse cuts a baby's umbilical cord to harvest cord blood. Using a patient's cord blood to treat cerebral palsy is based on the theory that the transfused cord blood's stem cells will travel to the brain and help repair and replace damaged brain cells.

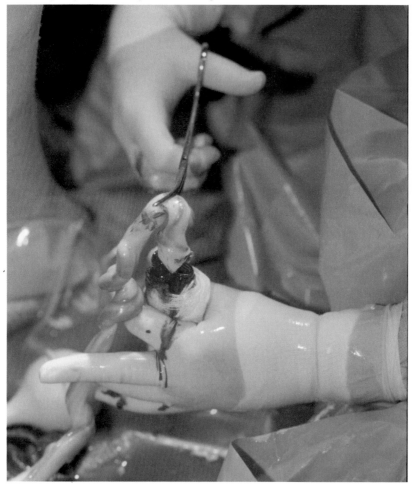

Using cord blood to treat disease is not uncommon. Cord blood stem cells have been proved to be an effective treatment in blood disorders, certain types of cancer, and bone marrow failure. Several laboratory studies have shown the cells' potential for reducing the effects of cerebral palsy. In a 2006 German study, scientists injured the brains of newborn rats, causing them to develop spastic cerebral palsy. Half the rats were treated with human cord blood. The other rats acted as the control. After the transfusion the rats that were treated with cord blood were able to walk normally, while the control group remained disabled. Next the rats' brains were examined. The researchers found that the stem cells had traveled to the treated rats' brains and incorporated themselves in the injured part.

Case studies involving humans have shown promising results, too. However, these studies did not include a control group, so the results are suspect. Therefore, in 2010 researchers at Duke University in Durham, North Carolina, began conducting a randomized controlled trial. In this study, the subjects were divided into two groups. Subjects in one group received an infusion of their own cord blood at the start of the study in September 2010. The second group received a placebo. The placebo group was scheduled to receive the infusion in July 2012. This method allows the researchers to use subjects in the second group as a control group from September 2010 to July 2012 without denying them treatment. Both groups' ability to move was monitored and compared for the duration of the study, which was scheduled to end in July 2013. Lead researcher Joanne Kurtzberg explains:

> We are very excited to have initiated this very important study, which will help us learn whether infusions of a child's own cord blood can lessen the symptoms of cerebral palsy. While there are many anecdotes [reports based on uncontrolled studies] suggesting that cord blood helps children with CP, it is essential to prove in a randomized trial, whether this is true. If this study shows that cord blood is beneficial, it will have a huge impact on the practices of cord blood collection and banking at birth.[29]

Dr. Joanne Kurtzberg, director of Duke University's Pediatric Bone Marrow and Stem Cell Transplant program, says the program's 2010–2012 study will find out just how much effect cord blood infusion has in treating cerebral palsy.

Many parents of children with cerebral palsy are not waiting for these results to seek out cord blood treatment. Cynthia and Derak Hextell are an example. Their son, Dallas, received a cord blood infusion in 2008. "It was such a drastic change within five days of the procedure taking place. . . . Before [the treatment] . . . we were trying to teach him to use a walker. Now he walks without assistance,"[30] the Hextells explain.

Whether or not the cord blood treatment was behind Dallas's improvement is not clear. What is clear is that people with cerebral palsy often combine a range of supportive therapies with their regular treatments in an effort to improve their muscle control and mobility. Some supportive therapies are widely accepted, whereas others are more controversial. It is up to individuals and their families to weigh the possible benefits of more controversial treatments against the possible risks, then make an informed decision.

CHAPTER FOUR

Facing Many Challenges

Living with cerebral palsy presents many challenges. There are a variety of ways individuals meet these challenges. In so doing they gain more independence and improve the quality of their lives. Neil Matheson puts it this way: "Some days, having a physical disability can be rough. Deep rough. Sometimes, I am like a frustrated golfer—after landing a shot smack in the middle of a difficult sand trap. But like any good golfer, I take a moment to recompose myself, acknowledge my handicap and, for better or worse, play on."[31]

Becoming More Mobile

Limited mobility is among the biggest challenges people with cerebral palsy face. Specially designed assistive devices help individuals meet this challenge. An assistive device is any device designed to compensate for, or enhance the function of, a disabled body part. Braces, walkers, and crutches are among the simplest assistive devices. Braces, also known as orthoses, act like splints. They support weak muscles, making it easier for individuals to sit and walk independently. They also stretch contracted muscles into more useful positions.

Braces can be worn on the feet, ankles, legs, hands, wrists, and torso. They may be made of metal, lightweight plastic, or neoprene fabric. To ensure a comfortable fit, braces are custom made and are replaced as the patient grows and the size and shape of their muscles changes. Even the best-fitting braces often feel cumbersome at first, but over time they come to feel more natural.

A teacher's assistant helps a child with cerebral palsy play T-ball with the aide of a walking device.

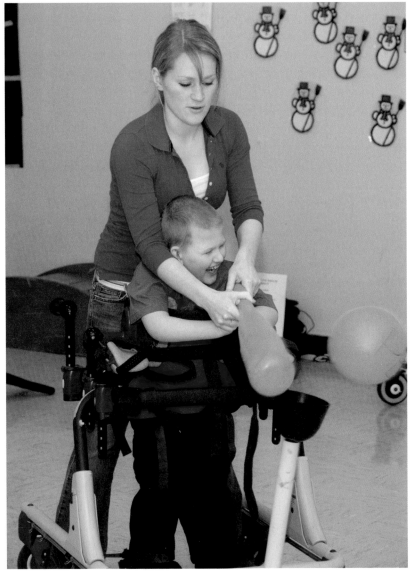

Foot, ankle, and leg braces usually extend around the wearer's foot. Most are worn in conjunction with a heel cup, a shoe insert made of plastic or a soft, padded material that keeps the wearer's foot flat inside a shoe. In some cases individuals must wear special orthopedic shoes with the brace. These are custom-made shoes that usually extend above the ankle, like high-top sneakers, with a rigid sole and sturdy construction to provide support to the foot. In other cases, patients can wear standard athletic shoes.

Some individuals with cerebral palsy increase their mobility by combining braces and a walker or crutches. Others are able to walk with the help of just one of these assistive devices. Walkers are especially useful for people who have poor balance. Walkers are made of aluminum or other lightweight metals and have four legs and two handlebars. Those for poor balance surround the user's back and sides. The user grasps the handlebars and takes a step, pulling the walker along. This helps the user get around more easily without depending on others to hold them up so they do not fall. Crutches, too, can give people with poor balance the support they need to walk without falling. Unlike traditional crutches that go under the armpit, forearm crutches are used by people with cerebral palsy. Forearm crutches have a ring through which the arm goes and a handle for the person's hand. This type of crutch provides users with the most stability. Matheson has been using forearm crutches most of his life. "Without crutches," he explains, "my balance isn't all that great."[32]

Wheelchairs

Walking is not an option for some individuals. Using a wheelchair helps these individuals move from place to place. There are many different types of wheelchairs designed to meet a variety of needs. The simplest are manual wheelchairs. They allow individuals who have use of their arms to propel themselves on solid terrain by moving the wheels with their arms. Special, small, super-lightweight wheelchairs are designed to accommodate children. Shahab, a boy with cerebral palsy,

A six-year-old with cerebral palsy uses a wheelchair in school. For cerebral palsy sufferers who cannot walk, motorized wheelchairs make them mobile and able to better participate in life.

recently got a lightweight manual wheelchair. With it he no longer has to depend on others to push him. "The old wheelchair was just so hard to maneuver and was so heavy," his mother explains. "Shahab couldn't push it that far himself because his arms got tired, but the new one is so light. . . . We can now all go out together as a family and don't have to worry about pushing Shahab anymore."[33]

An Inclusive Society

An inclusive society is one in which all people are included in all aspects of life. In her book *Only You Christine, Only You!*, disability-awareness professor Christine Komoroski-McCohnell talks about what such a society would be like:

> An inclusive country (or world) would insure that all banks, doctors' offices, restrooms, restaurants, subways, taxis, reception halls, museums, schools, universities, theaters, delis, buses, and so on, were completely accessible. . . . A ramp is not enough. A ramp is certainly a visible disability accommodation, but it's just a beginning. We also need doors that are at least thirty-six inches wide. Those doors must be easy to open, and not so heavy that folks with limited strength in their upper bodies can't open the . . . doors unless they are automatic. Talking elevators with Braille, as well as large print, Braille and picture symbols on menus, signs, and, well—everywhere! Recognition that service animals are not pets, and, as a result, these service animals must be allowed everywhere—not just as stated in the current laws, but in reality. Universal design in all new buildings which benefits everyone! Sign language, especially for all political discussions and debates, as well as snappy prime time TV shows.

Christine Komoroski-McCohnell. *Only You Christine, Only You!* Bloomington, IN: iUniverse, 2009. p. 92–93

Motorized wheelchairs propelled by small electric motors give people with limited use of their arms mobility. These wheelchairs can be controlled by a joystick, button, or switch mounted almost anywhere on the chair. This lets individuals control the chair with a push of almost any body part or even a puff of air. More sophisticated wheelchairs also contain a computer that works with the motor. In addition, voice-controlled wheelchairs are in development. An article on Cerebral Palsy and Technology, a website that explores how modern assistive devices can be used to help people with cerebral palsy, explains:

> The advent of the computer age has made it possible to create sophisticated wheelchairs which can give mobility back to those with poor motor control. If somebody has cerebral palsy and is unable to effectively propel or steer the wheelchair manually, they can still navigate thanks to the technology of switches and controls. Joysticks can be interfaced with the wheelchair's motor and computer in order to direct motion. In addition, switches are available for those who cannot manipulate a joystick. These switches come in a wide variety. Sometimes they are shaped like a button, and the push of a body part against the switch (such as a hand or foot) triggers an action, such as moving forward or turning. Other switches react to the presence of a body part, no touching is required. A wave of the hand or swing of the knee can activate these types of switches. But what if one's cerebral palsy makes it difficult to control their hand or knee enough to trigger these switches? They can still be mobile thanks to switches which respond to the position of the neck, head, and chin. Still other switches are manipulated by "sipping" and "puffing" air through a small straw. The sipping action will trigger the switch in one direction, and the puffing in the other. In "sip and puff" switches, often times the lips are used to control which direction to move in.[34]

Other specialty wheelchairs are designed to give individuals even more freedom. All-terrain wheelchairs, for example, have special large tires similar to those on mountain bikes. These chairs make it possible for disabled individuals to get around no matter the weather or the terrain. Individuals can use them off-road on dirt, sand, and snow. Sean, a boy with cerebral palsy, uses an all-terrain wheelchair. His mother talks about how it has enhanced his mobility: "The wheelchair solves my challenge of what to do with Sean in the wintertime. I didn't have a sled that could support Sean. We had the same problems at the beach. It's difficult to carry Sean onto a beach in the hot sun. . . . It's portable and the tires can handle snow and sand. Sean thinks it's the greatest thing. He feels like he's in a big monster truck."[35]

Elevated wheelchairs are another innovation. These wheelchairs are narrower than traditional wheelchairs. They can rise up and stand on two wheels, lifting their occupants into an almost upright position. This not only gives users better access to things around them, it gives them the psychological benefit of being able to talk and interact with nondisabled people face-to-face.

All these advances make it possible for individuals with even the most severe forms of cerebral palsy to become more independent. "Often I hear unknowing, able-bodied folks state that people with physical disabilities are 'confined' to wheelchairs," Christine Komoroski-McCohnell explains. "But are they really confined if they can freely move about an architectural space? To the person with mobility issues . . . a wheelchair is a device for freedom."[36]

Making Communication Easier

For people who have difficulty speaking, special devices known as augmentative communication devices make communication easier. Being unable to communicate effectively can be extremely frustrating. It isolates individuals, causes misunderstandings, and makes daily living difficult. Special communication devices help individuals meet these challenges.

Augmentative communication devices range from simple communication boards, in which children point to a picture of an object on a laminated card to express their needs, to high-tech computers equipped with communication software. Individuals touch pictures, letters, or words on the computer screen or use a mouse to point to words on the screen to select what they want to say. The most advanced software provides users with more than eight thousand words, phrases, and pictures to choose from. Selections are converted to speech by a synthesizer that can produce a natural-sounding human voice. Alex, a boy with cerebral palsy, went from a simple device to a sophisticated computer. When he started preschool he could barely communicate at all. He was taught to use a picture system in preschool in which he pointed to pictures to communicate his wants and needs. At five years old, he began using an augmentative communication computer. Once again he pointed to pictures, this time on the computer screen. The computer was programmed to speak his choices. Alex finally had a way to be heard. Next, he was introduced to a more sophisticated computer that offered

A child with cerebral palsy uses a Picture Exchange Communication System (PECS) device to participate in a class discussion. The use of these devices allows cerebral palsy patients greater social interaction.

him a more extensive vocabulary. His mother describes how it changed his life:

> He uses his computer to communicate his wants and needs at home. He can let us know what TV show he wants to watch, when he is hungry, when he is sick, and what is hurting. . . . Alex also uses his computer a majority of the day at school. . . . Alex is able to say the pledge of allegiance, tell jokes to his classmates, and sing happy birthday. . . . The other kids in his class all have their pictures on his computer and he can call them by name. It has increased his social interaction considerably.[37]

Other high-tech inventions allow people who cannot use their hands to use their eyes to communicate. A tiny camera mounted on top of a computer tracks the user's eye movements as they focus on vocabulary selections on the computer screen. Individuals are able to look at a phrase they want to say on the computer screen and blink, for example, to select it. The tracker connects to a speech synthesizer that converts the words into speech. It can also connect to a cell phone, so individuals can "talk" with friends at a distance. Users can also use their eyes to type on the computer, tweet, text, send e-mail, play games, surf the Internet, and participate in Internet chats and forums, which decreases their isolation and increases their social circle and independence.

Other devices, which are not designed specifically as augmentative communication devices, are also helping many people with cerebral palsy communicate more effectively. Tablet computers like the iPad, for instance, have speech applications, or apps, with predefined categories and phrases as well as a keyboard. Users can hold a conversation by typing in their thoughts, using the touch screen, or touching the speak button. The tablets are small, portable, and easy to use. In addition, since they are fairly commonplace, using them does not make individuals with cerebral palsy feel different. Glenda Watson Hyatt, an author, Web accessibility consultant, and blogger with cerebral palsy who can make sounds but cannot speak, explains:

The iPad can definitely be used as a communication device and is being used by thousands of people for that purpose. This time last weekend I was in Portland, Oregon, solo. Because of my iPad, I was able to communicate with the hotel front desk that my supposed wheelchair accessible room was not accessible. I was able to order a double cheeseburger and an iced mocha from McDonald's. I was able to carry on conversations with people I had just met.[38]

Accessibility

Even with the help of a variety of assistive devices, living in a world designed for nondisabled people is not easy for individuals with cerebral palsy. Even in their own homes, unintended barriers to movement can be challenging. Doorways, halls, and shower stalls are often too narrow to accommodate wheelchairs. Showers with a raised entry and houses with even a single step, not to mention an entire flight of stairs, can be an enormous barrier for people with limited use of their legs. Round doorknobs can be difficult for some individuals to turn. In addition, kitchens are often designed at a height that makes it impossible for a person in a wheelchair to access counters, cabinets, or the stovetop.

Making small modifications can greatly improve a person's ability to get around. Wheelchair ramps and handrails in hallways, as well as grab bars and seats in bathtubs and showers, can be helpful. Replacing hard-to-turn doorknobs with easier lever-style door handles can make a difference between dependence and independence.

Accessibility issues may also arise for individuals with cerebral palsy who want to drive but are unable to use their feet to operate an accelerator or brake pedal. Cars outfitted with special hand controls that allow people with cerebral palsy to drive without the use of their legs help individuals meet this challenge. Vehicles can also be equipped with retractable ramps that make it easier to move a wheelchair into and out of the vehicle. Adapting vehicles in this way can be expensive,

A car has been modified with a hand-operated pedal control
for a disabled driver. With these types of devices cerebral palsy
patients can drive a car just as well as anybody else.

but organizations such as the United Cerebral Palsy Association help link people in need to donors who help pay for
adapting vehicles. Being able to drive gives individuals with
cerebral palsy a lot of freedom. "I may talk and walk slow, but
I drive mighty fast," Komoroski-McCohnell admits. "While I am
behind the wheel, that's the only time I feel positively equal to
everyone else."[39]

Challenges in Public Places

Accessibility can also be a problem in public places. Despite the Americans with Disabilities Act, a federal law that requires that public places built after 1990 be accessible to the disabled, people with cerebral palsy still face many challenges. Aisles in older stores may be too narrow or cluttered to be accessible for people in wheelchairs. Groceries may be stacked too high to reach. Turnstiles and heavy doors in public places can be hard for handicapped people to access. Sports arenas, shopping malls, movie theaters, and subway stations may be so filled with fast-moving crowds that they leave individuals with poor balance vulnerable to being pushed over or knocked down.

A lack of benches in public areas and dressing rooms is another challenge for those who need to stop and rest or sit down while they try on clothes. Plus, even when accessibility is guaranteed, access may be denied, as it is when nonhandicapped drivers park illegally in spaces reserved for the handicapped. As new, more accessible buildings are built, however, and the public becomes more aware of the challenges handicapped individuals face, accessibility issues should improve.

Schools and the Law

Students with cerebral palsy face additional challenges in school, such as navigating crowded hallways, getting in and out of school chairs, taking notes, completing assignments and exams on time, raising hands, and carrying books. The Americans with Disabilities Act is one of a group of laws that help students with cerebral palsy meet these challenges. These laws require that all states provide education for children with handicaps, from ages three to twenty-one, and that students be educated in the least restrictive environment, which means in the most normal setting possible. These laws offer children under age three early intervention programs. They also provide students access to special transportation, equipment that makes learning easier, elevators and ramps, more accommodating chairs, reduced assignments, and extended deadlines,

Service Dogs

Service dogs can help individuals with physical disabilities live more independently. Service dogs can pull wheelchairs, help people keep their balance, and pull people up if they fall. They can carry items in their mouths or in backpacks and can retrieve items their owners drop. Some dogs can open and close doors by pulling a rope attached to the doorknob, switch on and off lights, press elevator buttons, fetch the phone, and bark if help is needed.

Service dogs are trained as part of special programs. Each animal is trained to work with a specific individual. Because of their intelligence, Labrador retrievers and German shepherds are often used. Would-be service dogs usually begin their training when they are about four months old. After about a year of training, the animals undergo an additional two to three weeks of training with their new owners. During this time, the owners learn how to command the dogs, and the owners and dogs begin to bond with each other.

It costs about twenty thousand dollars to train one service dog. These costs are paid for by charitable donations. Service dogs are provided free to people who need them.

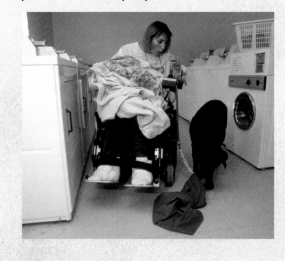

A service dog helps his disabled owner do laundry. Service dogs can be highly beneficial to a person with cerebral palsy. Each dog costs about twenty thousand dollars to train, however.

as needed. Often students are assigned an educational aide who takes notes for them and helps them move from class to class. Some students attend special-education classes, where they work with specially trained educators in a slower-paced environment.

Getting Support

Even with assistive devices and laws that aim to make life easier for people with disabilities, most individuals with cerebral palsy depend on a caring support network to help them cope with the many challenges they face. Support can come from many directions, including family and friends, personal care assistants, support groups, and virtual communities.

Personal care assistants are paid helpers who assist individuals with cerebral palsy do everyday tasks such as bathing, dressing, cooking, and housekeeping. Their help makes it possible for many adults with cerebral palsy to live independently.

Participating in a support group consisting of others with cerebral palsy also helps make daily living easier. Members provide each other with information and encouragement while sharing their thoughts and feelings. Working together, they are often able to come up with solutions to problems that individuals without cerebral palsy have difficulty understanding. Often members become close friends. There are also support groups for the parents of children with cerebral palsy, which help parents learn about new treatment options, assistive devices, and laws protecting their children. In addition, for those individuals that have difficulty attending support group meetings, there are electronic support groups that share information via the Internet. John W. Quinn explains: "The online social networking site Facebook has numerous support groups set up for people that have a friend or relative with CP [cerebral palsy]. It's a great place for anyone looking to share stories, common experiences, and get answers from people actually living with cerebral palsy. I have been able to connect with people from all over the world: London, South Africa, and Australia."[40]

The Internet also offers individuals a chance to connect with all kinds of people without their disability being an issue.

The social networking site Facebook has numerous electronic support groups for people who have or know someone with cerebral palsy.

Individuals can create avatars that can walk, talk, run, dance, or even fly to represent them in virtual worlds. People with disabilities can also join social networks, visit chat rooms, and author blogs in which they share thoughts, feelings, and the realities of their daily life with others.

Clearly, having a disability affects virtually every aspect of daily life. Assistive devices, laws aimed at helping people with disabilities, and a caring support network help ease the burden. Still, living with cerebral palsy can be challenging. By taking steps to meet the challenges they face, individuals with cerebral palsy improve the quality of their lives. Matheson explains:

> Everyone out there has a handicap of some sort. But not all handicaps are readily visible. My elbow crutches and bent legs are fairly noticeable. Other handicaps though, are harder to spot. Yet, in truth, we all have flaws. We all face obstacles, everybody struggles with something. It is our struggles that ultimately shape who we are and determine the person we will become. When adversity strikes, some people crumble. Others discover inner strength and perseverance to rise above it.[41]

CHAPTER FIVE

Looking Ahead

Much cerebral palsy research is focused on finding ways to prevent the condition from developing. While such research offers hope for the future, other research is focused on developing new treatments that improve the outlook for people who currently have cerebral palsy.

Brain Development

Scientists know that cerebral palsy is caused by mishaps in brain development. To better understand what happens when a fetus's or newborn's brain develops abnormally, researchers are studying normal brain development. They are examining how brain cells specialize, establish connections with each other, and become able to communicate with the body. Once researchers have this knowledge, they can work on ways to modify the effect of events that cause abnormal brain cell development, thereby preventing new cases of cerebral palsy from occurring.

To help gain more knowledge in this area, scientists at the University of California–San Francisco (UCSF) established the Newborn Brain Institute. There they are examining donated brains from babies and children who died from various causes, including brain injuries, between birth and age eighteen years. By comparing the brains and identifying brain cells at different stages of development, the scientists are able to trace brain cell growth patterns and the growth of neural connections. So far, they have learned that one area of the forebrain produces fewer new nerve cells after birth than other areas. If this area is injured by stroke or lack of air, for instance, it is less likely to repair itself and, as a result, the person is more likely to develop cerebral palsy. According to a report in the science journal *Nature*, "This type of data is crucial for understanding exactly what goes wrong when the brains of newborns are damaged. For instance, it is important to know whether stroke wipes out sources of new cells in the still-developing brain, or whether it prevents repairs to damaged cells, or causes damage through both mechanisms."[42] Once these questions are answered, scientists hope to develop ways to generate the production of new cells and/or repair damaged cells.

The cerebellum of a one-year-old. The Newborn Brain Institute at the University of California–San Francisco studies donated brains of infants to trace brain cell growth patterns and the growth of neural connections.

Lack of Oxygen and Dangerous Chemicals

Through studies of the brain, scientists have learned that lack of adequate oxygen can lead to an abnormal release of two otherwise helpful chemicals, lysophosphatidic acid (LPA) and nitric oxide, in a fetus's brain. In normal amounts these chemicals are important to brain development, but in excess they appear to damage developing brain cells. Therefore, scientists are looking at how these chemicals trigger brain damage and how this damage can be prevented.

In 2011 researchers at California's Scripps Research Institute examined the link between oxygen deprivation and LPA. LPA is a lipid, or fatty molecule. As a fetus develops, LPA acts as a signal that influences the creation of new brain cells, the way brain cells specialize, and their placement in the different regions of the brain. The importance of LPA in normal brain development led the researchers to theorize that the chemical might play a role in faulty brain development as well. To test their theory, the scientists analyzed what happened inside the brains of fetal mice that were deprived of adequate oxygen. Their findings showed that lack of oxygen caused increased LPA signaling, which caused brain cells to become overstimulated and die. In order to see if they could keep this from happening, the scientists deprived two groups of fetal mice of oxygen. One group was the control. The other group was administered a drug that blocked LPA signaling. Both groups' brains were then examined. The brains of those treated with the LPA blocker showed no damage, whereas the control group showed significant damage.

Future studies involving human brain cells are planned. If the findings are comparable, researchers hope to develop a medication, safe for humans, that would temporarily block LPA signaling in a fetus or newborn deprived of oxygen, thereby preventing the development of cerebral palsy. According to research team leader Jerold Chun, "Fetal brain damage from oxygen deprivation involves specific changes that are, surprisingly, mediated by this lipid signal called LPA. Because this pathway can be targeted with drugs, the discovery sug-

Gene Linked to Cerebral Palsy

Although cerebral palsy is not an inherited disease, it is possible that some individuals may be genetically predisposed to developing the condition. Researchers at Northwestern University in Evanston, Illinois, have found that a gene known as the E4 form of the Apolipoprotein E gene, which puts people at risk of developing Alzheimer's disease, may also make individuals more susceptible to cerebral palsy. The researchers took genetic samples from 418 children, half with cerebral palsy and half without, which they analyzed and compared. The subjects who carried the E4 gene were three times more likely to have cerebral palsy than those who did not carry it. They were also more likely to have a more severe form of cerebral palsy than the subjects with cerebral palsy who did not carry the gene.

As a result of these findings, it is likely that in the future, medical professionals may test infants at risk of developing cerebral palsy for the gene. If they carry it, the babies will be given early intervention therapy even before they show signs of cerebral palsy.

gests that creating new medicines that target LPA receptors may be a way of limiting or preventing serious developmental brain diseases."[43]

In 2009 other scientists at Northwestern University in Evanston, Illinois, investigated the link between oxygen deprivation, excess nitric oxide, and brain damage. Nitric oxide is found in brain cells, where it acts as a neurotransmitter, a chemical that helps brain cells communicate with each other. It is also found in other cells in the body, where it helps regulate blood pressure and the immune system. At normal levels nitric oxide is essential to wellness. However, when a fetus is deprived of adequate oxygen, the brain overproduces nitric oxide; high levels of this chemical injure developing brain cells. To prevent such damage, the researchers developed two

compounds that inhibit the production of nitric oxide in the
brain. The compounds had to be highly selective, targeting the
brain without interfering with the production of nitric oxide in
other parts of the body.

The scientists tested the compounds on three groups of
pregnant mice. One group acted as the control. The other two
groups were treated with one or the other compound. After
treatment, the oxygen supply between the mother and the
fetuses was diminished in all three groups. The results were
quite promising. None of the newborn mice treated with either
compound died, whereas more than half of the untreated animals died. Of the treated animals, 83 percent treated with one
compound showed no signs of cerebral palsy, and 69 percent
treated with the other compound showed no signs of the condition. There was no damage to either treated group's blood
pressure or immune system.

The researchers are working on perfecting the potential
drugs. They are hopeful that the medication may one day be
used to prevent cerebral palsy from developing. Researcher

A brain researcher prepares brain tissue to study an oxygen-
deprivation link to cerebral palsy.

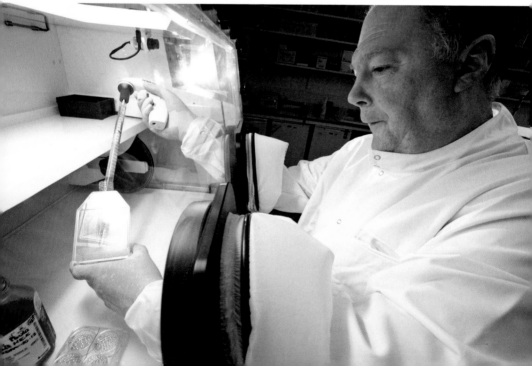

Sidhartha Tan explains: "We still have to bring the phenomenon to humans, which would be very exciting. There is such a dire need. If we could safely give the drug early to mothers in at-risk situations, we could prevent the fetal brain injury that results in cerebral palsy."[44]

Maternal Infections and Brain Development

Other scientists have been working on developing a way to prevent fetal brain damage that occurs as a result of maternal infection. When an individual gets an infection, the immune system releases powerful chemicals known as cytokines. Cytokines cause inflammation, redness, swelling, and heat, which helps fight infection. Cytokines can pass from a mother's bloodstream into a fetus's brain. Although they are essential to healing, cytokines can interrupt and damage fetal brain development.

In 2010 researchers at the University of California–Berkeley theorized that treating pregnant mothers who have an infection with magnesium sulfate would prevent cytokines from damaging fetal brain cells. Magnesium sulfate is routinely given to women to stop preterm labor. A 2008 University of Alabama–Birmingham study found that children whose mothers were treated with magnesium sulfate during labor were less likely to develop cerebral palsy than children whose mothers received a placebo. It is not known why or how magnesium sulfate protects preterm babies. "We knew there were indications from other studies that magnesium sulfate might protect a preterm fetus from cerebral palsy, but we wanted to demonstrate direct and conclusive protective effect on the offspring brain in cases of maternal inflammation,"[45] explains head researcher Ron Beloosesky.

With that goal in mind, Beloosesky and his team administered an infectious agent to a group of pregnant rats. A second group acted as the control. The rats in both groups were randomly treated with magnesium sulfate or a placebo. Twenty-five days after birth, all the pups' brains were examined by magnetic resonance imaging (MRI) scans. The brains of the

Magnesium sulfate, or common Epsom salt, has been found to reduce the chance of cerebral palsy when mothers take it during labor.

offspring of the rats that were administered an infectious agent and were treated with a placebo showed brain injury, whereas the offspring of the uninfected rats and of the infected rats treated with magnesium sulfate showed no injury. The researchers plan further studies in hopes of learning exactly how magnesium sulfate protects the fetal brain. Based on their findings, it is likely that in the near future, pregnant women who contract an infection will be treated with magnesium sulfate to help protect their babies from developing cerebral palsy.

Premature Births and Brain Injuries

Since more than 10 percent of babies born prematurely have brain injuries that lead to cerebral palsy, other researchers are focusing their attention on the role the placenta plays in brain development and whether being cut off from the placenta prematurely causes problems in the brain. The placenta is a thick layer of cells that surrounds the fetus. It is expelled from a woman's womb when she gives birth. For a long time, scientists thought that the placenta's only functions were protecting the fetus and allowing food and oxygen to pass to the fetus. But recent studies have shown that the placenta produces a number of hormones that help direct fetal brain development. Hormones are chemicals that control and regulate the activity of different cells and organs. Some hormones appear to be produced late in pregnancy. Scientists theorize that when premature infants are cut off from the placenta, their brains do not receive the instructions that these hormones provide and therefore are unable to develop normally. According to Anna Penn, a neonatologist (a medical doctor specializing in newborn infants) at Packard Children's Hospital in California, "Without the placental signposts, development is hobbled. If we can figure out exactly what directions have been lost, we can chart an identical map and help keep development on course."[46]

In an effort to do just that, Penn turned off one hormone gene at a time in genetically engineered mice to see which hormones were produced late in pregnancy and which had the biggest impact on brain cell development. She also collected blood samples from premature and full-term human babies and compared the hormones found in the blood of each group. By 2010 she had pinpointed two hormones that reach their peak levels late in pregnancy—progesterone, which helps brain cells grow, and oxytocin, which protects brain cells from damage.

Once scientists know more, they hope to be able to measure a premature infant's hormone levels at birth and replace what is missing, thereby ensuring that the infant's brain will continue to develop normally.

Recent studies show that the placenta (red, upper left) not only supplies food and oxygen to the fetus but also produces a number of hormones that help direct fetal brain development.

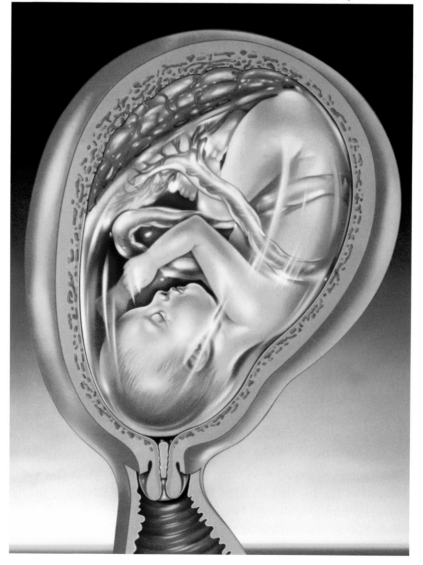

Antibiotics and Premature Labor

Another study is investigating whether there is a link between administering antibiotics to pregnant women in premature labor and the development of cerebral palsy. Currently, when women go into premature labor they are routinely administered an antibiotic. This appears to delay the onset of labor, and it protects them from developing an infection. However, a British study that began in 2001 and ended in 2011 indicated that administering antibiotics in this way may raise the chance of the baby developing cerebral palsy.

The study involved 4,221 pregnant women in danger of premature labor. Some, but not all, of the women's water had broken; that means the amniotic sac around the baby had ruptured, which happens shortly before a woman gives birth. The women, none of whom had an infection, were randomly treated with an antibiotic or a placebo until they gave birth, for a maximum of ten days. As a follow-up, in the next ten years 3,196 of their children were examined for signs of cerebral palsy. The results were startling. For the women whose water broke early, taking antibiotics did not affect their children. However, the risk of developing cerebral palsy roughly doubled for the children whose mothers took antibiotics before their water broke, compared to those whose mothers did not. Researchers are unclear why the study showed such a significant increase in cerebral palsy cases among the children whose mothers took antibiotics before their water broke, and more studies are planned. In the meantime, in an effort to prevent the development of cerebral palsy, many medical professionals are being more cautious about prescribing antibiotics to healthy women in danger of going into premature labor.

New Treatments

While some researchers are working on ways to prevent cerebral palsy, others are developing new treatments. One experimental treatment being tested at the UCSF neurological nursery unit focuses on premature infants who may have experienced a traumatic event such as lack of oxygen, strokes, or seizures before, during, or after birth. The treatment involves a cooling method that appears to arrest or reverse brain damage. The idea for the treatment, which is known as hypothermia treatment, came from animal studies in which laboratory subjects were exposed to lack of oxygen during birth. Half the subjects' bodies were cooled, lowering their body temperature by a few degrees. The other half was the control group. Then the subjects' level of brain damage was measured and compared. Those who received hypothermia treatment had much less damage than the control group. Scientists are not sure why this was so. They know that lowering a mammal's body temperature lowers its need for oxygen. They theorize that lowering the brain's need for oxygen makes it easier for damaged brain cells to recover and stops further damage.

In the treatment at the UCSF, premature babies are placed on special pads that have coils containing cold water circulating through them. The cold water lowers the babies' body temperature to 92.3°F (33.5°C). The babies are kept on the pads for three days. During this time, the babies' brain activity is closely monitored via electrodes that are placed against their skulls and attached to a computer, and the babies are kept sedated and fed intravenously. On the fourth day the water in the pad is heated, and the babies' body temperature is gradually warmed until it returns to normal. At that point the newborns are taken in incubators to an MRI machine, where a medical professional conducts a brain scan. After being released, the babies are monitored for the next three years. The results of a study of 325 babies who received the treatment are promising. Forty-four percent of the babies show no brain damage or signs of cerebral palsy, compared with 28 percent in the control group who received regular intensive care treatment.

Although the treatment is still in its experimental stage in the United States, it is becoming more common in Europe and South Africa. If ongoing research proves the value of the treatment, it is likely to become more common in the United States, too.

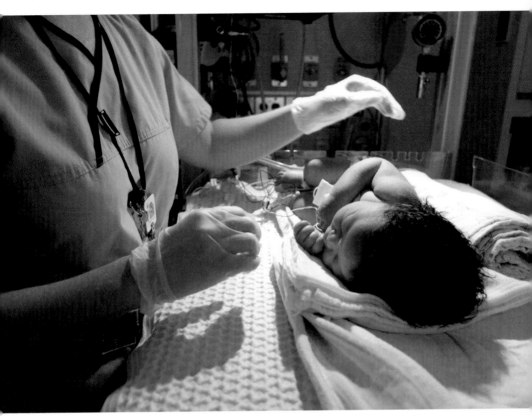

An intensive care nurse adjusts the hypothermia treatment cooling blanket on a newborn. Hypothermia treatments change how a baby's brain reacts to injury.

Electrical Stimulation

Another developing treatment uses electrical stimulation administered in a new way to loosen tight muscles. It involves the use of slight, practically undetectable electric impulses to stimulate tight muscles and help them relax. Studies have shown that such treatment can help. Scientists are unclear about why it does. They theorize that the electric impulses replicate nervous impulses that damaged brain cells would otherwise produce. Electrical stimulation treatment for cerebral palsy has been available for many years, but the method of delivering the electrical pulses was complicated, which made the treatment less common. It required that patients be implanted with expensive, bulky devices by a surgeon or have electrodes connected to lead wires placed on their skin by a trained medical professional. Patients had to remain still during treatment.

Researchers at the National Institute of Neurological Disorders and Stroke in Bethesda, Maryland, developed a high-tech delivery system, which makes the treatment simpler. The new treatment uses a hypodermic needle to inject tiny wireless devices that produce electrical impulses into spastic muscles. The devices are controlled and powered by a telemetry wand that works like a remote control. It directs the number and strength of the electrical pulses.

Robotic Therapy

Scientists at the Massachusetts Institute of Technology (MIT) are investigating another high-tech treatment method: using robotic technology to help people with cerebral palsy gain better control of their arms so that they can reach for and grasp objects more easily. The treatment is based on the theory that if certain pathways of the brain are damaged, other pathways may open up and become stronger with repeated use. Consequently, it should be possible to rebuild brain connections damaged by cerebral palsy by using a robotic device that repeatedly guides the user's arm to perform specific tasks.

The scientists tested the treatment on stroke patients first and achieved excellent results. In 2009 they began experimental treatment on children with cerebral palsy. During the treatment, patients put their lower arm and wrist into a brace attached to the arm of a robotic joystick. A video screen displays simple tasks for the patient to perform. It is a lot like playing a simple video game, except if movement does not occur, the robotic joystick moves the patient's arm. If the patient moves the joystick in the wrong direction, the robot gently moves his or her arm in the right direction. Movements must be repeated hundreds of times to be successful.

The results of three experimental treatment studies have been excellent. Patients have increased their ease and speed of movement. Other experimental treatments are now being done using similar robotic equipment to help children with cerebral palsy learn to walk. As a result of the treatment, some patients who could not walk without assistance are able to walk independently. According to Joelle Mast of Blythedale Children's Hospital in Westchester County, New York, where some of the experimental treatments are being done, "The research that has been done with robotics is really exciting. . . . We have seen in our initial studies gains that were completely unexpected. . . . Results are very promising. I think there is tremendous hope for cerebral palsy."[47]

A paralysis victim uses robotic legs to help her learn to walk. Robot technology allows people with cerebral palsy to better gain control of their limbs.

Summer Camps for Young People with Cerebral Palsy

Summer camps sponsored by organizations like the United Cerebral Palsy Association give children and teens with cerebral palsy an opportunity to make new friends and have fun participating in activities with special equipment that strengthens their muscles. These activities include swimming, horseback riding, boating, fishing, soccer, acting, music, and arts and crafts, to name just a few. Campers are paired up one-on-one with a counselor or volunteer who works with them, helps them with their personal needs, and keeps them safe. All the while, campers have fun with young people like themselves.

The camps may be day camps or residential overnight camps. Campers who cannot afford the cost may get financial help from the sponsoring organization. Research has shown that attending summer camp helps young people with cerebral palsy to feel more independent, improve their self-confidence, and develop physical and social skills.

It is likely that in the near future, robotic treatment will be another option for people with cerebral palsy. In the meantime, researchers at MIT are working hard to develop more robotic therapy equipment to help people with neurological disorders. In fact, they are developing a physical therapy center entirely equipped with robotic treatment devices.

Although there still is no cure for cerebral palsy, researchers like those at MIT offer real hope. As scientists learn more about the brain and how it develops, there is hope that many if not all cases of cerebral palsy will be prevented in the future. Until that time, new treatments should help improve the lives of people with cerebral palsy now.

Notes

Introduction: Reaching Their Potential

1. Robert Reid. *Bursting with Life*. Knoxville, TN: Koinonia, 2010, p. 15.
2. John W. Quinn. *Someone Like Me*. Palisades, NY: History, 2010, pp. 20–21.
3. Christine Komoroski-McCohnell. *Only You Christine, Only You!* Bloomington, IN: iUniverse, 2009, p. 26.
4. Reid. *Bursting with Life*, p. 17.
5. Quoted in Diane Hales. "Who Says I Can't?" United Cerebral Palsy, July 27, 2003. http://affnet.ucp.org/ucp_channel doc.cfm/1/15/64/64-64/5084.
6. Neil Matheson. *Daddy Bent-Legs*. Winnipeg, MB: Word Alive, 2009, p. 3.
7. Komoroski-McCohnell. *Only You Christine, Only You!*, p. 29.

Chapter One: Understanding Cerebral Palsy

8. Quinn. *Someone Like Me*, p. 36.
9. Quoted in Ellen. "Kids with Special Needs Around the World." *Love That Max* (blog), July 16, 2010. www.love thatmax.com/2010/07/kids-with-special-needs-around -world.html.
10. Matheson. *Daddy Bent-Legs*, p. 43.
11. Katy Fetters. "A Flashback on Cerebral Palsy." Teen Cerebral Palsy, October 24, 2010. www.teencerebralpalsy .com/cerebral-palsy-help.
12. Quinn. *Someone Like Me*, p. 21.
13. Wai Kin Chiu. "Information Technology and Persons with Disabilities Conference." Seattle Schools. http://sps.seattle schools.org/schools/hale/friends/hkspeech.html.
14. René Z. Milner. "Frustrations of Mild Cerebral Palsy." Come Unity. www.comeunity.com/disability/cerebral _palsy/mildcp.html.

15. Monica Videnieks. "Communication Not Lacking in This Relationship." *Accent on Living*, Summer 2001, p. 66.

Chapter Two: Diagnosis and Treatment

16. Quoted in Centers for Disease Control and Prevention. "Learn More About Cerebral Palsy." www2c.cdc.gov/pod casts/media/pdf/CerebralPalsy.pdf.
17. Quinn. *Someone Like Me*, p. 34.
18. My Child. "Therapy for Cerebral Palsy." http://cerebral palsy.org/about-cerebral-palsy/therapies.
19. Reid. *Bursting with Life*, pp. 22–23.
20. Ellen. "Serial Casting Success: This Time the Miracle Stayed." *Love That Max* (blog), July 6, 2011. www.lovethat max.com/2011/07/serial-casting-success-this-time.html.
21. St. Louis Children's Hospital. *Selective Dorsal Rhizotomy.* www.stlouischildrens.org/content/medservices/About SelectiveDorsalRhizotomy.htm.
22. Quoted in *Sun* (London). "I'll Walk You Down the Aisle Mummy." September 4, 2009. www.thesun.co.uk/sol/home page/woman/real_life/2635332/Miracle-spine-op-for-cerebral -palsy-boy.html.

Chapter Three: Supportive Therapies

23. Mary C. Vrtis. "Sam and His Horse." Suite 101, May 27, 2007. http://mary-c-vrtis.suite101.com/sam-and-his-horse -a21570.
24. Jan Vilums. "Aquatic Therapy for Children with Cerebral Palsy." Healthy Times Online. www.healthytimesonline .com/archives/aquatic_therapy_cerebral_palsy.html.
25. Erica Cao. "Music Therapy for Cerebral Palsy: The Carter School." *The Artistic Synapse* (blog), March 16, 2011. http://theartisticsynapse.blogspot.com/2011/03/music -therapy-for-cerebral-palsy-carter.html.
26. Quoted in Susan L. Kaplan. "Ben's Plastic Brain." *Exceptional Parent*, August 2010, p. 48.
27. Tara. Comment on Ellen. "The Death of Dee Spears: Can Botox Injections Hurt Your Child?" *Love That Max* (blog),

January 28, 2010. www.lovethatmax.com/2010/01/death-of
-dee-spears-could-botox.html.

28. Ellen. "The Death of Dee Spears."

29. Quoted in Duke Transitional Medicine Institute. "Kurtzberg and Team Move Forward with Cerebral Palsy Cord
Blood Study." www.dtmi.duke.edu/news-publications
/news/dtmi-news-archives/kurtzberg-and-team-move-for
ward-with-cerebral-palsy-cord-blood-study.

30. Quoted in Bob Considine. "Amazing Recovery Attributed
to Cord Blood." *TODAY* Health, March 11, 2008. http://to
day.msnbc.msn.com/id/23572206/ns/today-today_health/t
/amazing-recovery-attributed-cord-blood.

Chapter Four: Facing Many Challenges

31. Matheson. *Daddy Bent-Legs*, p. 57.

32. Matheson. *Daddy Bent-Legs*, p. 11.

33. Quoted in Debbie Andalo. "Social Mobility." *Guardian*
(London), July 8, 2008. www.guardian.co.uk/society/2008
/jul/09/disability.children.

34. Cerebral Palsy and Technology. "Mobility." http://comput
ers-technology-cerebralpalsy.com/cerebral-palsy-mobility
.html.

35. Quoted in Becky Rodia. "The Power of Fun: A Chance
Meeting Between an Engineering Professor and an 11-Year-
Old Boy with Cerebral Palsy Led to the Creation of Five
Devices That Enhanced the Child's Life." *Exceptional Par-
ent*, September 2009, p. 56.

36. Komoroski-McCohnell. *Only You Christine, Only You!*,
p. 76.

37. Lynn Trinrud. "Alex and His Computer." *Exceptional Parent*, July 2010, p. 64.

38. Glenda Watson Hyatt. "Teachers, Don't Take Away the
Child's Voice." *Glenda Watson Hyatt* (blog), September
25, 2011. www.doitmyselfblog.com/2011/teachers-dont
-take-away-the-kids-voice.

39. Komoroski-McCohnell. *Only You Christine, Only You!*,
p. 36.

40. Quinn. *Someone Like Me*, p. 198.

41. Matheson. *Daddy Bent-Legs*, p. 58.

Chapter Five: Looking Ahead

42. Erika Check Hayden. "Neuroscience: The Most Vulnerable Brains." *Nature*, January 13, 2010. www.nature.com/news/2010/100113/full/463154a.html.

43. Quoted in *Science Daily*. "Discovery Suggests Way to Block Fetal Brain Damage Produced by Oxygen Deprivation." September 1, 2011. www.sciencedaily.com/releases/2011/09/110901142625.htm.

44. Quoted in Megan Fellman. "Stunning Finding: Compounds Protect Against Cerebral Palsy." Northwestern University, February 24, 2009. www.northwestern.edu/newscenter/stories/2009/02/cerebralpalsy.html.

45. Quoted in *Women's Health Weekly*. "Study Finds Magnesium Sulfate May Offer Protection from Cerebral Palsy." February 24, 2011, p. 335.

46. Quoted in Jeneen Interlandi. "The Prematurity Puzzle." *Newsweek*, November 1, 2010, p. 42.

47. Quoted in MIT Department of Mechanical Engineering. "Robotics New Hope for Cerebral Palsy." Video. Massachusetts Institute of Technology, May 19, 2009. http://web.mit.edu/newsoffice/2009/robotherapy-0519.html.

Glossary

assistive device: Any device designed to compensate for or enhance the function of a disabled body part.

ataxic cerebral palsy: A type of cerebral palsy causing problems with balance and coordination.

athetoid cerebral palsy: A type of cerebral palsy causing loose muscle tone and involuntary movement.

augmentative communication device: An assistive device that makes communication easier.

cerebellum: The part of the brain that coordinates balance and the sequence and duration of movement.

cerebrum: The part of the brain that controls thought, among other things, and contains the motor cortex.

constraint-induced movement therapy: A form of intensive physical therapy aimed at reorganizing and reprogramming the brain.

cord blood: The blood inside the umbilical cord.

diplegia: A term used to describe spastic cerebral palsy affecting both arms or both legs.

fetus: An unborn baby.

hemiplegia: A term used to describe spastic cerebral palsy affecting the arm and leg on one side of the body.

monoplegia: A term used to describe spastic cerebral palsy affecting one limb.

motor cortex: The part of the brain that helps control voluntary movement. It is located inside the cerebrum.

muscle tone: The stiffness or looseness of a muscle.

neurons: Nerve cells that send and receive electrical signals throughout the body.

placenta: The organ that connects the developing fetus to the uterine wall. It protects the fetus and allows food and oxygen to pass to the fetus through the umbilical cord.

plasticity: The ability of the brain to develop new pathways to replace injured pathways.

premature birth: A birth that occurs before the end of the normal nine-month-long pregnancy.

prenatal: A term used to describe the period before birth.

quadriplegia: A term used to describe spastic cerebral palsy affecting all four limbs.

spastic cerebral palsy: A type of cerebral palsy causing stiff, tight muscles.

spinal cord: The thick bundle of nerves that extends from the brain down the back. It carries information from the brain to the muscles, carries sensory information to the brain, and coordinates certain reflexes.

stem cells: Cells that are capable of changing into and repairing any cell in the body.

stroke: Bleeding in the brain.

Organizations to Contact

Cerebral Palsy International Research Foundation

1025 Connecticut Ave. NW, Ste. 701
Washington, DC 20036
Phone: (202) 496-5060
Website: www.cpirf.org

This organization sponsors cerebral palsy research. It offers information, fact sheets, and videos on cerebral palsy.

Children's Hemiplegia and Stroke Association

4101 W. Green Oaks Blvd., Ste. 304
PMB 149
Arlington, TX 76016
Phone: (817) 492-4325
Website: www.chasa.org

This association provides information, news, and support for people with hemiplegia. It sponsors support groups and on-line discussion groups.

March of Dimes Birth Defects Foundation

1275 Mamaroneck Ave.
White Plains, NY 10605
Phone: (914) 428-7100
Website: www.marchofdimes.com

This is one of the largest organizations working to improve the health of babies. With chapters throughout the United States, the March of Dimes provides information and sponsors research on birth defects, premature births, and pregnancy issues.

National Institute of Neurological Disorders and Stroke (NINDS)

PO Box 5801
Bethesda, MD 20824
Phone: (800) 352-9424
Website: www.ninds.nih.gov

This institute is part of the National Institutes of Health. Its goal is to help people with neurological disorders. It sponsors and conducts research and provides information and the latest news on brain research.

United Cerebral Palsy Association

1660 L St. NW, Ste. 700
Washington, DC 20036
Phone: (800) 872-5827
Website: www.ucp.org

This national organization provides information and support for people with cerebral palsy and their loved ones. It publishes newsletters and informational pamphlets and sponsors research and summer camps. There are local chapters throughout the United States.

For More Information

Books

Rita Carter, Susan Aldridge, Martyn Page, and Steve Parker. *The Human Brain Book*. London: DK, 2009. This book examines the brain, including how it develops and works. It contains lots of diagrams and pictures and a section on movement and muscle control.

Jacqueline Langwith, ed. *Perspectives on Diseases & Disorders: Cerebral Palsy*. Farmington Hills, MI: Greenhaven, 2011. A collection of articles presenting information on cerebral palsy, new research, different points of view about controversial treatments, and personal experiences.

Sarah Levete. *Explaining Cerebral Palsy*. Mankato, MN: Black Rabbit, 2010. A look at what cerebral palsy is, including its causes, diagnosis, management, and the challenges it presents.

Robert Snedden. *Understanding the Brain and the Nervous System*. New York: Rosen, 2010. This simple and colorful book explains how the brain and nervous system are constructed and how they work.

Periodicals

Jerome Groopman. "A Child in Time." *New Yorker*, October 24, 2011.

Doug Most. "Physical Therapy." *Runner's World*, August 2010.

Dana Puglisi. "Interview: The Unlikely Hero: Q&A with John W. Quinn, Senior Chief Petty Officer, USN (ret.)." *Exceptional Parent*, September 2010.

Emily Ledbetter Viguers. "Swimming for Function." *Rehab Management*, Fall 2010.

Pam Woody. "Against All Odds: Not Even Cerebral Palsy Could Keep This Youngster from Riding, Competing, and Winning." *Horse & Rider*, October 2011.

Internet Sources

KidsHealth. "Cerebral Palsy: Keith's Story." http://kidshealth.org/teen/diseases_conditions/brain_nervous/keith_story.html.

National Institute of Neurological Disorders and Stroke. "Cerebral Palsy: Hope Through Research." www.ninds.nih.gov/disorders/cerebral_palsy/detail_cerebral_palsy.htm.

Websites

Cerebral Palsy and Technology (http://computers-technology-cerebralpalsy.com/index.html). This website provides information about different assistive devices designed to help people with cerebral palsy, including the latest high-tech innovations.

Reaching for the Stars (www.reachingforthestars.org). The website of this nonprofit organization offers information about cerebral palsy, including videos and interviews with people with cerebral palsy.

Treating Cerebral Palsy (http://treatmentofcerebralpalsy.com/index.html). Provides information about a wide range of traditional and less conventional treatments for cerebral palsy.

Index

Picture Credits

Cover: © Huntstock, Inc./Phototake. All rights reserved.
© AP Images/Brian Kersey, 39
© AP Images/Elizabeth Dalziel, 52
© AP Images/Karen Tam, 56
© AP Images/Steven Senne, 46
© AP Images/The Daily Progress, Andrew Shurtleff, 85
© Brian Mitchell/Alamy, 21
© BSIP/Photo Researchers, Inc., 17, 35
© Charles D. Winters/Photo Researchers, Inc., 80
© Christina Kennedy/Alamy, 32
© Cynthia Tunstall/Alamy, 54
© Ellen B. Senisi/Photo Researchers, Inc., 8, 30, 59, 61, 65
Gale/Cengage Learning, 15, 23
© James King-Holmes/Photo Researchers, Inc., 78
© Janine Wiedel Photolibrary/Alamy, 48
© John Bavosi/Photo Researchers, Inc., 82
© Justin Sullivan/Getty Images, 87
© Olivier Voisin/Photo Researchers, Inc., 51
© Petit Format/Photo Researchers, Inc., 75
© Picture Partners/Photo Researchers, Inc., 27
© Scott Camazine/Alamy, 19
© Simon Fraser/Photo Researchers, Inc., 12
© Spencer Grant/Photo Researchers, Inc., 68, 70
© Tom Ervin/Getty Images, 43
© Universal Images Group via Getty Images, 37
© Urbanmyth/Alamy, 72

About the Author

Barbara Sheen is the author of more than sixty books for young people. She lives in New Mexico with her family. In her spare time, she likes to swim, walk, garden, and read.